MONSTERS OF OLD LOS ANGELES

Also by Charles M. Martín

ONCE A COWBOY

ORPHANS OF THE RANGE

MONSTERS OF OLD LOS ANGELES

*The Prehistoric Animals
of the La Brea Tar Pits*

BY CHARLES M. MARTIN

Illustrated by Herb Rayburn

THE VIKING PRESS · NEW YORK · 1950

To JOHN HERMAN, D.SC.

Whose abundant knowledge and untiring assistance made this book possible.

Charles M. Martin

Second printing September 1951
Third printing July 1955
Fourth printing September 1958
Fifth printing October 1961

Copyright 1950 by Charles M. Martin
First published by The Viking Press in August 1950
Published on the same day in the Dominion of Canada
by The Macmillan Company of Canada Limited

Printed in the United States of America

CONTENTS

	Acknowledgments	7
	Foreword	9
1.	The Sage of the Ages	13
2.	Eat to Live	20
3.	Primordial Supremacy	29
4.	The Stampede	38
5.	A New Home	45
6.	Life at La Brea	52
7.	Ricky Arrives	58
8.	Ricky and Racky	67
9.	The Rains Come	74
10.	The Miracle of Life	81
11.	The Greatest Tragedy	88
12.	Six-Ton Mother Love	95
13.	Thanksgiving Day at La Brea	103
14.	The Land of Plenty	110
15.	Go West, Young Man!	117
	Addenda: The La Brea Excavations	125

ACKNOWLEDGMENTS

I wish to make grateful acknowledgment to those scientists who helped me so unselfishly while I was doing the research and writing of this book.

To Dr. John Herman, whose encouragement and untiring energy helped so much in gathering the factual material while I was doing the field work, and also at the Los Angeles County Museum. Dr. Herman worked closely with me on the correlating of the prehistoric animals with the forms of similar species which exist today in various parts of the world. He was a bulwark on which to lean for all geographical locations as well, which is far afield from his usual pursuits, in his long and illustrious career as a chemist.

To Dr. Chester Stock, Senior Curator of Science at the Los Angeles County Museum, who directed much of the more recent exploratory excavation work at La Brea. Dr. Stock's book, *Rancho la Brea* (Science Series No. 11, Paleontology No. 7), furnished much of the factual material.

To Dr. Hildegarde Howard, Curator of Avian Paleontology, for her assistance in ascertaining information regarding the birds and plants of ancient La Brea. Some of the leaves and small seeds were found in the skulls of mice which had been preserved in the tar pits for forty thousand years, and from such minute evidence Dr. Howard identified many of the forms of plant life of the Pleistocene period.

ACKNOWLEDGMENTS

To Dr. John A. Comstock, now retired, but who for years was Senior Curator at the Los Angeles County Museum, for his splendid cooperation and many helpful suggestions.

To Doctors Merriam, Miller, and Kerr, who have been credited for their discoveries by Dr. Stock in his Science Series.

Also my grateful thanks to the directors of the Los Angeles County Museum, and particularly to Dr. James H. Breasted, Jr. The opportunity to study the restorations at the Museum was an invaluable aid.

My heartiest thanks to Captain George Allan Hancock, who donated the acreage containing the La Brea Pits to the County of Los Angeles in perpetuity for the public, for his many philanthropic services in making the restorations possible. Captain Hancock donated La Brea to the County in 1913, in memory of his late father, Major Henry Hancock.

The explorations in Hancock Park were started by Dr. Merriam and his associates of the University of California in 1913. All the pits are plainly marked to give the student of the prehistoric animals of La Brea much priceless information.

To Herb Rayburn, talented young artist, who accompanied me on my research work to the fields and museums, and who made many sketches of the material in Hancock Park and in the Hancock room in the County Museum. His gifted talent helped clothe many of the skeletal remains with the flesh of reality for this book.

To these, and to the staff members of the Los Angeles County Museum who gave so graciously of their time and knowledge, I wish to express my most sincere appreciation.

CHARLES M. MARTIN

FOREWORD

To many of us closely associated with the sciences, it seemed that there had long been a need for a story of the animals and life of old La Brea, a story told in the terms of the layman, so that it would be clearly understood by the other millions of laymen who have been fascinated by the fossil remains of prehistoric animals taken from the tar pits.

Thousands of students from the high schools and colleges of Southern California are taken to the La Brea pits, and to the Los Angeles County Museum, to study this wonderful collection. These students search eagerly for knowledge concerning the prehistoric animals, and are especially interested in how the animals appeared in the flesh, forty thousand years ago.

It has been my pleasure to be with Mr. Charles M. Martin on most of his field trips and in the museums and libraries while he was conducting his research for this book. No slightest detail was too insignificant for him to explore and study.

It was most interesting to watch him compare the prehistoric fossils and their restorations with the present forms of recent animals—such as the lionlike cat with the African lion, the ancient bison with the modern form, the ancient mammoths with present-day elephants.

Mr. Martin makes no attempt to speak in the complicated terms of the scientists, although he does give the scientific names in his footnotes. He tries to tell a realistic story of life at the tar pits of forty thousand years ago, in what is now the heart of modern Los Angeles.

The resulting story is amazingly lifelike in its interpretations, a story in which the author used what factual material was available, coupled with his trained ability as a creative writer.

I feel that American literature will be enriched by this story which has long been needed to balance the findings of those learned scientists who have worked for more than thirty-five years to produce the La Brea assemblage.

Mr. Martin has written a book which should be of interest to those of every age group, and especially to students of Paleontology. The magnificent collection of fossil remains at the Los Angeles County Museum will be more readily understood after a careful reading of this word-picture created by an author who is well known to most of you.

JOHN HERMAN, D.SC.

May 6, 1949

MONSTERS OF OLD LOS ANGELES

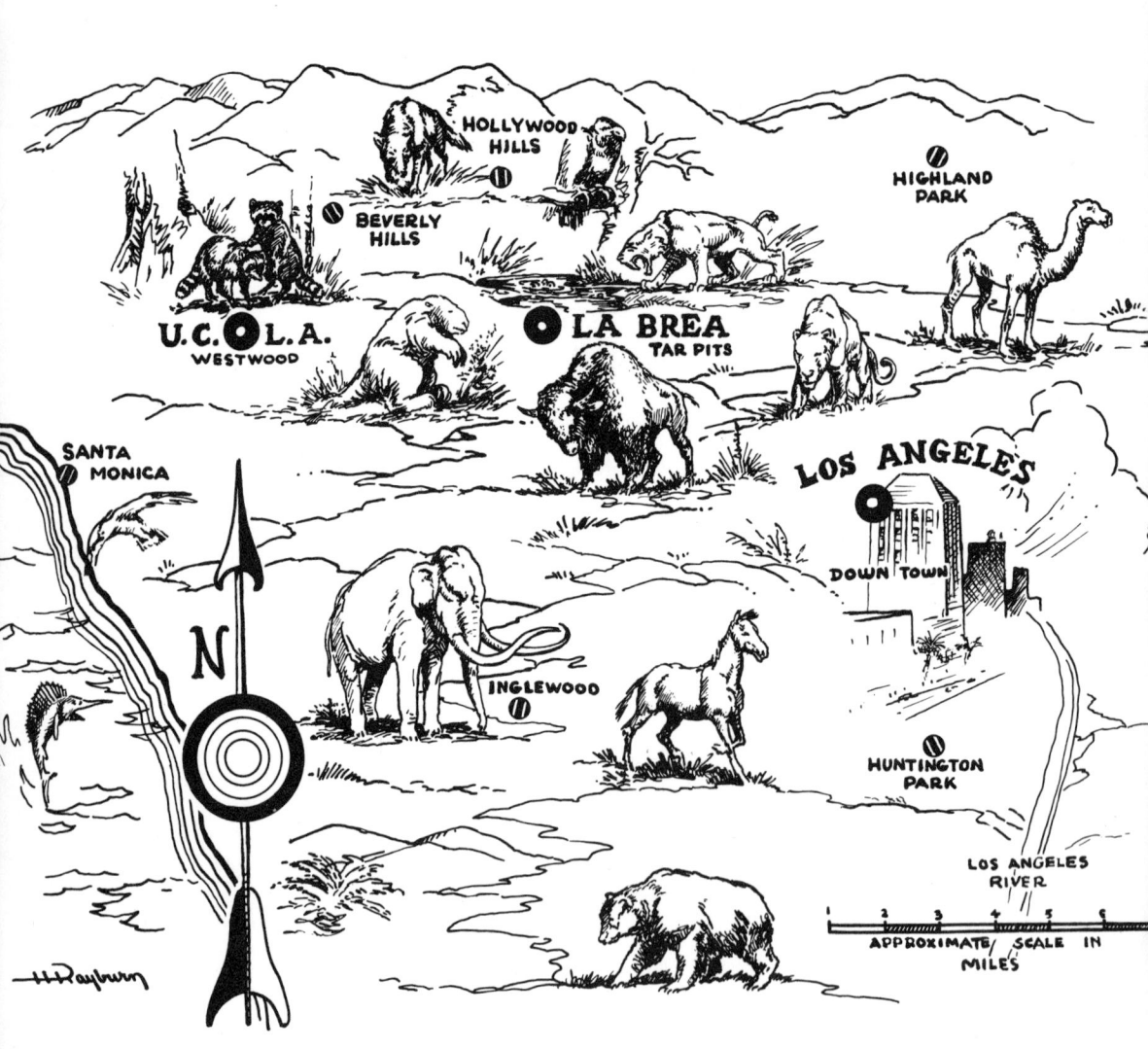

I. The Sage of the Ages

Nature was kind to the Southern California of forty thousand years ago, during the Pleistocene era. Vegetation was lush and plentiful, the annual rainfall averaged fifteen inches, and the climate was much as it is now.

Nature nearly always gives a vague warning of impending disaster to those who have learned to look and listen. The creatures of the wild had *felt* the gradual change that was taking place almost imperceptibly. A vast migratory movement was in progress from north to south, toward the low hilly country and the vast coastal plains surrounding what is now modern Los Angeles.

A gradual change was taking place in the climate of North America. Far out in the south Pacific, great volcanoes were erupting on the barren islands. Thick clouds of dust filled the air, obscuring the sun, drifting with the prevailing winds. Perhaps our solar system passed through cosmic clouds, depriving a part of the earth of heat energy. This was the beginning of the Ice Age, and, perhaps being warned by a sixth sense, the animals were moving south where the climate was temperate and food more abundant.

A herd of wild horses[1] thundered through Cahuenga Pass from the Hollywood hills. Something had frightened the fleet-footed animals, which now sought safety out on the open plains.

A small furry gray body moved with cautious stealth through the high coarse bunch grass on a small hillock that commanded a view of the low feeding grounds. A pair of round wise eyes peered out from the grasses with which the animal blended perfectly.

There was a wistful expression on the small wrinkled face of the quiet observer who saw all, heard all, and said—nothing. The sage of the ages had come to Los Angeles, but the sage was lonesome. This was Racky, the astute raccoon.[2]

Racky watched the startled horses which faced toward the north. A great stallion stood apart from the herd, his domed head held high with nostrils flaring wide. The prevailing wind was from the west. It brought a tang of salt air from the Pacific Ocean, twenty miles to the west, but it also brought something else.

The wise raccoon wrinkled up his nose and sniffed inquiringly. He detected a strange odor—a pungent, oily smell. The little animal stiffened and then squatted down behind the grass-shrouded hillock as a vague feeling of unrest warned him of a hidden danger.

The wild horses began to graze on the coarse lush grass near a small stream. Only their leader remained alert and on guard. The stallion faced a distant copse of live oak trees growing in a depression that was surrounded by a heavy growth of tall grass.

The raccoon flattened out when the tops of the distant grass moved slightly. The great stallion pricked his ears forward and whistled softly in his throat. The grazing herd lifted their heads at the warning,

1. *Equus occidentalis*
2. *Procyon lotor*

and then the stallion was among the mares, driving them westward with flashing, snapping teeth.

The horse herd raced across the great plains in full flight while Racky crouched in his sheltered hiding place. The raccoon turned his gaze back to the copse of trees.

His wise eyes widened with recognition when the grasses moved violently. A great tawny head came into view, followed by a crouching muscular body, as a giant carnivore padded into the clear.

Racky watched with frightened interest. The crouching animal was the largest and strongest of all the flesh-eating predators which made up the Felidae family, the great lionlike cat.[3]

A second tawny form leaped out from the high grass, landed lightly on padded paws, growled softly in her deep throat, and then started in swift pursuit after the herd of horses.

From his secure vantage point Racky watched the pair of great cats streak across the plain, shoulder to shoulder. The wistful expression of loneliness grew more pronounced on the raccoon's expressive face. The stallion has his band of mares; the great lion had his own mate. Somewhere in this great new land of plenty there *must* be another raccoon.

Now the stealthy pair of lions were mere specks in the westward distance. Racky left his hiding place and followed the broad spoor left by the fleeing horse band. He kept to the shelter of the abundant bunch grass until he came to the borders of the small running stream.

Hunger assailed Racky when he discovered a succulent root which had been uncovered by the churning hoofs of the frightened horses. Grasping the root in his small front paws, which were very much like tiny hands, the raccoon dipped the food in the flowing stream and washed it thoroughly.

3. *Panthera atrox*

What other animals did to their food was no concern of Racky's. Cleanliness was inherent in him; he *always* washed every bit of food before breaking his fast. He would do his hunting at night for the most part, but he was in a strange land.

It was late afternoon when Racky reached the area where trees grew abundantly. The strong, oily odor again assailed his sensitive nostrils, and he crept into a burrow of overhanging grass to investigate. His motto seemed to be "*Look before you leap,*" and every fiber of his being seemed to vibrate to warnings of unseen danger.

Racky saw a tuft of grass move about twenty yards to the right of his hiding place. A giant flat-footed hare[4] hopped into the clear and stopped to glance cautiously in every direction, then dropped down on all fours and hopped away.

Racky made himself thin on the ground in the sheltered burrow as a swift, lancing shadow slanted out from overhead. A shaft like molten yellow metal streaked toward the unsuspecting hare, and Racky's warm blood turned cold when he recognized a great golden eagle.[5]

The monarch of the air struck once, but fiercely. The hare bleated shrilly as the vicious curved beak severed the spinal cord at the back of the neck. Huge taloned claws gripped the limp hare as strong wings stirred the air furiously, and Racky saw the eagle rising higher and higher in the clear blue of a flawless turquoise sky.

The great bird alighted on a rocky shelf near a tall pine tree[6] and began to tear the skin from the dead hare.

The raccoon shuddered and looked for an avenue of escape. His nose wrinkled with repugnance as the westerly wind carried the

4. *Lepus timidus*
5. *Aquila chrysaetos*
6. *Pinus muricata*

pungent oily odor across the low pocket, and he started toward higher ground where clusters of rocks afforded some measure of shelter.

His progress was slow because of his extreme caution, and his shaggy head lifted when he came to a small pool of water. Instantly the raccoon retreated and skirted the innocent-looking pool. A few iridescent bubbles floated on the surface of the water, carrying the same unmistakable oily odor of uncleanliness to Racky's flaring nostrils.

Again a shadow warned him from above, and Racky sought refuge in a tiny cave. He heard the beat of wings coming closer, and then a long-legged stork[7] hovered over the tiny pool. Slowly the great wings folded, and the stork alighted in the small pool to drink.

Racky watched with cunning interest. A deep wrinkle appeared between his wide eyes when the stork took a forward step. The foot emerged for an instant, covered with something black and sticky, but the other foot refused to move. The long-billed stork gave a raucous cry as it floundered and beat the pool with its outspread wings. The raccoon watched in silent wonder.

The terrified bird was beating the turgid water with flailing pinions and its cries of terror filled the late afternoon air. No longer did the trapped stork stand erect, and as the beating wings rose and fell they were covered with a black sticky substance which dripped from the drooping feathers in a glistening shower.

Too frightened to move, the raccoon watched the struggle through fear-widened eyes. Now the odor of pungent oil was very strong, and Racky realized that only his instinctive cleanliness had saved him from a like fate.

The cries of the stork were now feeble, and the flapping of the powerful wings became less. Tiny bubbles appeared on the surface

---

7. *Ciconia maltha* Miller, after Howard

of the pool, grew larger, and burst with little crackling noises. The odor of oil became still more pronounced as the hapless stork sank deeper into the viscous mass until only the beak and parts of the wings were visible.

Racky shuddered and drew back into the twig-covered burrow. He turned midway, crept to the back end, and emerged in an animal run which led to higher ground. He had had his first sight of the tragedy of La Brea,[8] the tragedy of the tar pits.

Twilight was settling over the land when Racky made his stealthy way up a low hill which was covered with volcanic rock. There were convenient pockets in the event that it became necessary to seek instant shelter. At long last Racky found a deep hole and worked his way into it until only the tip of his sharp nose was visible. From under bushy eyebrows, his gleaming black eyes stared out over the land which was now shrouded by a brooding silence, dissipated by the early call of nocturnal insects.

Only those dark eyes moved as Racky studied every bit of the strange terrain. He had no way of knowing that the movement of the glacial ice had caused him to leave his home in the north. It would require slow and careful study of this new land to learn of the unknown dangers, but after he had learned, he would adapt himself to his surroundings.

His eyes watched familiar forms in the near distance toward the north. He recognized the wild horse band grazing on the plains by a small stream. Suddenly he stiffened. He also recognized something else when a tawny head lifted above the tall bunch grass to the east of the grazing horses.

The stallion leader was on guard, but the wind was blowing from

8. "The tar"

the northwest, and this prevented the horse from detecting the scent of the huge lionlike cat. The lion withdrew into the dense brush, but Racky followed the slight movements of the grasstops with wise and understanding eyes.

A pair of lions were moving to attack from the north, and the pungent odor of oil came from the south. The unsuspecting horses would be between the great predatory beasts and the tar traps, and when they attempted to escape—

The raccoon quivered and continued his silent vigil. He remembered the helpless stork, the miring, slimy tar, the fate of the nimble hare.

As the shadows lengthened over La Brea the noises of the crickets became more pronounced. Occasionally the call of an owl sounded weirdly through the semi-silence of the forbidding gloom.

Racky stared across the plain at the grazing horses. He saw the great stallion suddenly throw up its head, and then came a shrill blasting whistle of warning. The feeding horses jerked up their heads and faced the north, poised for instant flight.

2. Eat to Live

The tule-like grass crackled loudly as two tawny forms burst through the outer fringe. The startled horse herd snorted and raced toward the south after one terrified glance at the great lionlike cats.

The hair behind the raccoon's neck raised in a great ruff as terror almost froze his blood. What he had seen once, that he would always remember. Racky was thinking about the long-legged stork in the tiny pool of tar. He turned his head slowly to follow the flight of the stampeding horses. Beyond them, and perhaps half a mile to the south, Racky could see the glistening water on larger pools. Here and there a large cypress[1] stood in majestic silence, its great branches overhanging the dark forbidding pools. He could also make out the shadowy shapes of several huge birds roosting in the trees—waiting and watching. He had seen the great vultures in lazy flight, with wing-spreads of fourteen feet.[2] Now they rested above the tar traps, their large

1. *Cupressus marocarpa* Hartweg
2. *Teratornis merriami* Miller

heads cocked wisely to one side, their strong and rapacious bills gleaming dully like short curved scimitars.

In another tree he saw several lesser birds, somewhat smaller in size than the awesome Teratorni. These were also vultures,[3] scavengers of the air.

From his high point of vantage Racky watched the flight of the terrified horses and the pursuit of the hungry lions. Most of the horse band had skirted to the west of the trees by instinct. They knew from long experience that the big cats could crouch on overhanging limbs above a water hole and drop down on the backs of their defenseless victims.

There is little difference between *Equus occidentalis*, the horse of the Pleistocene era, and the Western horse of today. It averaged about fifteen hands in height, weighed approximately a thousand pounds, but the skull was slightly domed, and the hoofs were perhaps a third smaller than those of our present horses.

The lionlike cats were larger than the African lion of today, weighing as much as eight hundred pounds. They were swift in pursuit for short distances, deadly in combat, and could break the neck of a horse with one powerful blow of a huge front paw.

Racky crouched in his tiny cave, watching the flight of the terrorized horses. Several of the stragglers on the fringe of the stampede were crowded under the cypress trees, and then they were in the pools, throwing up sprays of glistening water.

The huge vultures stirred sluggishly but did not leave their perches. Four horses were in the large pool under the trees; the rest of the band were far away toward the near-distant ocean.

The ruff stiffened on the neck of the watching raccoon as two tawny

---

3. *Gymnogyps amplus* Miller

shapes streaked through the coarse grass. The smaller of the pair was the female. The male lion launched his muscled body at a struggling horse on the margin of the pool. The cruel claws bit deeply into the glossy hide of the horse, and a paw swung viciously to strike the horse on the dome of the skull.

One startled scream shattered the air under the shadow-shrouded cypress. The horse sagged down, churning the water and the tar beneath it. The body, rolling sluggishly, carried the lion into the pool, where he wallowed frantically, seeking a foothold in the petroleum slime.

The female lion waited on the firm earth, watching the struggles of her mate. He was roaring with furious anger, but his cries of rage changed gradually to screams of terror. A young horse, not much more than a colt, came charging through the trees in search of his mother. The old mare was struggling frantically ten yards out from the edge of the pool.

The lioness made a lunge and slapped with a paw at the same time. The colt went down under the blow with scarcely more than a grunt, and the female lion disemboweled the kicking colt with one savage rip of her razor-sharp claws.

There was a litter of cubs to feed back in the Hollywood hills, and the maternal instinct was ever uppermost. As the lioness lowered her muzzle to sniff the kill, a low savage growl sounded just off to one side, in the deep shadows of the cypress tree. Instantly the lioness faced the sound, her lower lip snarling back to show the huge canine teeth in the front of her capacious mouth. The ruff stood up angrily behind her head, and the lean belly was drawn up by sheaths of muscles which now made ready to spring.

Recovering from the fright which had rendered him temporarily immobile, the raccoon crept out of the cave to the trunk of a dead cypress tree. Using his hands and the clutching toes of his hind feet, he scuttled up the scaly tree trunk like a small agile bear. He listened intently at a hole in the decayed trunk, and then crept into the hollow and quickly turned. Now he had a splendid position from which to watch the snarling monsters on the ground, some twenty feet below.

Racky's eyes glowed redly. Now he knew what had disturbed the lioness; what had distracted her attention from the kill. The stiff hairs began to crawl on his back.

Crouching beneath the cypress upon which the giant vultures were perched was an awesome-looking monster. Although not so large as the lionlike cat, the crouching beast resembled the lioness in many respects. Two large teeth like curved sabers were prominent in the upper jaw, one at each side of the mouth. The tail was shorter than that of the lioness, but the color of the hide was almost the same. This was the saber-tooth cat.[4]

The saber-tooth cat was moving toward the lioness and her kill, and just behind the intruder was another of the same species. Both were snarling savagely, crouched low to the ground, and maddened to an almost insane rage by the smell of the fresh blood of the slain young horse.

Racky flattened out in the tree trunk, scarcely daring to breathe. The murky gloom of twilight had given way to the deeper shades of night.

The trapped horses had ceased to struggle. The male lion was moving feebly; only half-closed eyes gleamed to tell of life, and then the big head lolled and sank beneath the sticky slime.

4. *Smilodon californicus* Bovard

The snarling lioness galvanized to frenzied activity after that first pause of stunned surprise. She sprang at the male saber-tooth cat, which rose to meet her from an almost flat, crouching position.

The sudden lunge put the lioness on top as the two beasts reared up, locked in a deadly embrace. The saber-tooth cat threw his head back to get leverage and swing for the stab with its powerful canine teeth. The sharp sabers were at least six inches long, but they did not find their mark.

The lioness sank her teeth into the exposed throat of the saber-tooth cat, thrusting the smaller animal's head well back. Powerful forefeet ripped tawny flesh to shreds as the huge carnivores fought to the death.

The female saber-tooth cat made no effort to help her mate. She crept up to the body of the dead colt and began to feed on the carcass, seemingly indifferent to the fate of her spouse as he fought a losing battle for his life.

Now the two gladiators were down, with the saber-tooth cat underneath. The lioness nudged with a powerful thrust of her neck and shoulders, found the jugular vein, and jerked back savagely.

The saber-tooth cat gasped and slumped over in a limp heap. For a few seconds the lioness watched the dying spasms of her foe, and then the hungry growls of the female saber-tooth caused her to swing around, facing the dead colt.

One tremendous leap carried the lioness through the air toward the interloper. Her right paw lashed out as she passed over the saber-tooth cat, and the sharp claws ripped the hide from the smaller cat's forehead. It also knocked her sprawling from the prey, but the saber-tooth turned instantly to meet the attack.

The lioness landed on all fours and whirled swiftly. The saber-tooth

had launched an attack of her own, and the deadly sabers stabbed into the flesh on the right side of the lioness.

The two beasts fell apart and then came to grips, with forepaws clawing each other as they reared up on powerful hind legs. Again the superior height and weight of the lionlike cat began to tell. She forced her lighter opponent to give ground, and the saber-tooth fought desperately with the weapons with which nature had provided her. She struck down with the twin sabers, her lower jaw dropping, her mouth widely agape.

The lioness snapped at the pendulous lower jaw, twisting her head and body to the side as she followed through to avoid the gleaming sabers.

The saber-tooth cat screamed in agony as her lower jaw was broken and almost torn from her skull. The lioness rolled up and cuffed viciously, sending the wounded saber-tooth sprawling. She was after her stunned victim as the saber-tooth tried to roll up, and the lioness caught a grip behind the head, in the vertebrae of the neck. One savage jerk broke the saber-tooth's neck and also flung the writhing body far out into the tar pit. The mortally wounded cat landed on a slimy island which was the half-submerged body of a dead horse and slithered off into the viscous ooze.

The lioness now turned toward the slain colt, growling low in her throat. She seized the dead horse by a front leg and dragged the carcass back from the edge of the treacherous tar pit. Then she ripped hide from a shoulder and bit out a large chunk of flesh.

From high up on his perch above the pool the raccoon watched with eyes that were wise with the wisdom of the ages. He heard the lioness dragging the carcass of the dead horse away. He knew that she would eat her fill and then take a hind quarter to her cubs in some hidden cave deep in the Hollywood hills. The rest would be left for the scavengers, which even now were skulking from the deeper shadows.

Racky saw a huge black shape take form as it approached the margin of the pool, where the front legs of an old mare rested on the firm bank; the rest of the animal was mired deeply in the asphalt.

EAT TO LIVE

The shape approaching was the dreaded dire wolf,[5] with which Racky was familiar. The terrifying beast held its huge head low, and seemed to have scarcely any neck. Strong shoulder muscles joined the head to show that the dire wolf could exert tremendous pulling power. The strongs jaws and great teeth gave a warning that *Canis dirus* could crush a very large bone.

The big wolf bunched his feet and tugged mightily. The mired mare moved slightly. From the shadows another wolf joined the first, seized the other front leg of the mare, and added her weight to the pull.

The mired body began to move and left the tar with a loud, sucking sound. The two wolves began to snap at the front legs of the mare, the only parts of the carcass which were not covered with petroleum slime.

Farther back in the deep shadows the raccoon could see the skulking forms of a lesser breed of wild dog. These were the true four-footed scavengers, the cowardly coyotes.[6] They would eat what their larger cousins left, after satisfying their hunger.

Now the raccoon saw a strange thing. The huge dire wolves had gnawed the forelegs from the dead horse and had retreated to the deeper shadows. Racky could hear them crunching bones with their immense and powerful jaws. The air began to stir as nature sent her air-borne forces to do their work.

The giant Teratorni had left their perches in the big cypress tree. They floated to earth on wide-spread wings and came to rest on the body of the slain horse.

Racky watched the huge vultures rip the slime-covered hide with their powerful beaks, exposing the firm red flesh to the light of a sickle moon which had just slanted up from behind the low hills.

5. *Aenocyon dirus* Leidy
6. *Canis orcutti* Merriam

A dozen of the huge birds were ripping the slimy hide from the carcass of the slain horse. Great hunks of meat were shoveled into the lower jaws by the powerful beaks of the big birds, and then nature had her way again.

A series of low, warning growls sent the great vultures back to their perches in the cypress. The two huge dire wolves rushed from the shadows and began to devour the meat which the vultures had skinned out for them. When they had gorged themselves, the wolves slunk back into the shadows.

Now the coyotes came on with a rush, making the night air hideous with their echoing screams. The mare was soon reduced to scattered white bones.

The sickle moon rose high in the sky. The musical notes of crickets again took up their symphony. Little bubbles of gas formed far out on the surface of the tar pit, grew in size, and burst with popping or sucking noises. The tragedies at La Brea were not new and had been often repeated.

3. Primordial Supremacy

The night forces of nature hovered over the tar pits of old La Brea with a brooding melancholy. Tiny sucking noises came from the bursting gas bubbles in the petroleum slime, against an overtone of sound made by the nocturnal insects.

The great Teratorni stirred fitfully in ,the cypress tree, clicking their horny bills to dislodge vagrant morsels of flesh from the weaker lower part of the mouth structure. Now the black vultures[1] were busy, tearing the flesh from the broken bones of the male saber-tooth cat.

Racky listened from his perch high above the fearsome pool. He cocked his head forward when a gnawing sound reminded him of his own hunger. He recognized those noises, made by field mice and by other small rodents. With scarcely a sound to tell of his passage, Racky left his perch and descended the scaly bark of the dead tree.

He looked like a very small bear as he reached the ground and paused to listen. Eternal vigilance was the price of survival. His body was covered with coarse grayish-brown hairs, and his long furry tail was ringed alternately with bands of black and white. He had short

1. *Coragyps occidentalis* Miller

ears and a sharp nose, wide intelligent eyes, and feet that were more like tiny hands.

Racky remembered the forelegs of the mare which the dire wolves had dragged back away from the pool. He hugged the base of the tree as he peered through the stygian gloom with eyes that could see in the dark because of his natural nocturnal habits.

A large white bone loomed plainly in the darkness near a clump of low verdure. Bunch grass offered a screen as Racky advanced stealthily toward the leg bone of the slain mare. He made no sound as he hugged the ground, and the gnawing noises of the rodents became louder.

Racky paused behind a clump of grass and peered between the intertwining grasses. A family of mice were gnawing at the fresh bone.

The hungry raccoon gathered his legs beneath him, held his head low, and leaped upon the feeding mice. His two front paws reached out and gripped a pair of plump mice, which squealed just once.

Racky flattened out on the ground, with all his senses tuned for any warning of danger. Then he ambled along the ground in the deeper shadows. He sniffed inquiringly when he came to a depression which was filled with clear spring water. When he was satisfied that the water was clean, and that there was no immediate danger from some other hunter of the night, he washed the mice thoroughly in the cold clear water.

Perhaps it was this habit of cleanliness which was responsible for his longevity, and for the continuance of his species. The raccoon had lived down through the ages when more powerful creatures had become extinct; he was destined to survive when most of his contemporaries of the Pleistocene had disappeared in antiquity.

With his hunger partially satisfied, and his thirst slaked, Racky moved away from the sweet spring. He darted to the side when some mysterious sense alerted him to danger. Swishing wings brushed him lightly, and a curved beak scratched his neck vertebrae as a red-tailed hawk[2] missed his strike by scanty inches. Then the raccoon darted into a rabbit burrow, his heart pumping madly.

This was the law of the wild, where the hunter so often became the hunted. Even while he was breathing hard, Racky heard a clicking, snapping sound, and the startled, half-stifled scream of the great hawk. Before turning to make a cautious investigation, Racky knew what had happened.

Peering from the sheltered depth of the burrow, Racky saw a lean gray fox[3] dragging the stricken hawk into the underbrush. The raccoon ruffled slightly and remained quiet for several minutes while he identified all the night noises around and above his shelter.

When a scud of clouds passed in front of the waning moon the raccoon left the rabbit burrow and moved stealthily toward the hole in the dead tree. He climbed the scaly bark just as the cloud banks floated eastward across the pale moon. After pausing briefly at the entrance to the hole to make certain an intruder had not pre-empted his new home, Racky climbed in and curled up to watch the strange life of La Brea.

From the near-distant Hollywood hills he could hear the eerie echoing calls of the coyotes, the scraping sounds when the giant condors sought for a more secure grip on the cypress branches with their great talons; the incessant gnawing of rodents among the bones at the margin of the treacherous tar trap.

The raccoon stared out over the pool, wrinkling his sensitive

2. *Buteo jamaicensis*
3. *Urocyon californicus* Mearns

nostrils as the pungent odors from the bubbling gas mingled with the fog floating in from the sea, across the vast coastal plains. He would move to a more acceptable abode after he had oriented himself to the strange new land, but for the present Racky was grateful for the protective shelter of the ancient dead tree.

The long night passed slowly and became a part of the past. The false dawn threw off the shackling shadows of night for a brief time—that elusive half-light between night and day, when the night is dying, and a new dawn is not yet born. It would last for a few moments only, after which the forces of darkness would again hold sway until the sunrise.

Racky peered over the rim of his nest when a grunting noise came from the tall coarse grasses at the west margin of the pool. Except for a few bubbles, the pool might have contained stagnant water. Every creature had to have water for survival.

The raccoon identified the grunting noise instantly. He knew that one of the largest mammals was seeking forage and drink—the giant sloth,[4] which moved very slowly but with irresistible power. The beast was sitting up on tremendous, column-like hind legs, the feet of which terminated in long claws. The powerful front legs were also armed with long claws, turned slightly inward. The great beast was using its long powerful tail to make a tripod, and it was licking at the foliage of low trees with a long red tongue, grunting as it fed on the grasses and leaves within reach. Huge grinding teeth could be seen as the sloth opened its powerful jaws, and the obese body was covered with coarse light brown hair.

The great sloth made no attempt at secrecy as it foraged for food. The lesser creatures of the Pleistocene seldom attacked the two-ton

4. *Paramylodon harlani* Owen

monster. Many had been killed in the fights arising mostly over the right-of-way, but the carnivorous beasts did not like the flesh of the sloth and ate it only when forced by starvation, in order to survive.

The false dawn faded as quickly as it had come, and now all of nature seemed in a state of suspended animation, as though waiting for the new day. Brooding silence again shrouded the tar pits, and even the ever-present gas bubbles seemed silent, gathering strength and size.

A faint glow appeared in the east, and a bird cheeped sleepily as it stirred. The sun burst suddenly above the low ring of hills and was met by a feathered chorus of joyous welcome.

Racky stretched his neck and peered over the edge of his nest to see what the giant sloth was doing. His eyes widened as a tearing, rending noise announced the coming of another giant, striding through the heavy underbrush as if it had been only coarse grass.

Racky knew that this was not the coming of another sloth; they never hurried and had little wit for anything except the elemental processes of simple living. This new sound heralded the approach of some powerful and dominating creature: a creature that knew where it was going and what it was going to do after it had arrived.

Fascinated by the sounds, Racky leaned forward to watch. The giant sloth continued to feed, and Racky sniffed inquiringly when he saw the sloth in a clump of bushes which were heavy with dull brown berries.[5]

The sounds became louder the nearer the stranger came to the feeding grounds. A heavy swale of grass was crushed to earth as a huge tall form appeared suddenly from the dense underbrush, a creature so powerful that it dwarfed the giant sloth until the sloth straightened

---

5. *Celtis mississippiensis* Bosc

up. Then they were almost of a size. Racky watched with interest as the drama began to unfold. The newcomer was the great short-faced bear.[6] On all fours, the monster stood four feet high at the shoulders, and twice that height when he reared up suddenly on his hind legs. The heavy neck was drawn down into the muscle sheaths of the huge shoulders, with the powerful front paws held ready to strike from either side.

Racky watched unwinkingly as the startled bear stared at the giant sloth. Huge ripping claws taloned from the bear's great paws, and a savage roar of anger erupted from his deep cavernous chest.

The bear's body was covered with coarse dark-brown hair which glistened as the great muscles contracted spasmodically. Long canine teeth curved inward as the bear opened his mouth to growl, but the sloth moved sluggishly and continued to feed.

The great bear never yielded the right-of-way to any living creature, and it was evident that he had no intention of changing the fixed habits of a lifetime. The hackberries were a luxury to him, and it was evident that he meant to brook no opposition to his appetite.

The bear took a forward step and growled a warning. The sluggish sloth continued to feed, shoveling in the brown berries from the near branches with the claws on its front legs, chewing slowly with its heavy grinding teeth.

The sloth was perfectly balanced on its two hind legs and huge hair-covered tail. Small gleaming eyes watched the threatening bear jealously, but the sloth depended on its great size for protection.

Suddenly, and without warning, the short-faced bear moved swiftly forward and slashed out with a swinging clawed left paw. The blow caught the sloth on the side of the head and upset the tripod balance.

---

6. *Tremarctotherium simum* Cope

Before the sloth could recover, the bear slapped viciously with the right paw.

The sloth uttered a strangled, gasping roar as the blows sent it reeling backward. Blood was dripping from the lacerated powerful jaws as the sloth rolled over and rose up on its strong hind legs. It moved back to the berry thicket and reached for a heavily laden branch, but the fruit was never carried to those waiting jaws. The great bear moved in and came to grips with the sluggish sloth. The sloth instinctively sought for a grip with the powerful claws on its front legs, and the bear was trying to get his paws around the gross body of the giant sloth.

As the claws of the sloth ripped into the flesh of the bear, a blinding anger exploded in the bear's brain. His huge head came forward with jaws agape, and the long canine teeth ripped savagely at the exposed throat of the bleeding sloth.

The bear pressed forward with the leverage of his tremendous hind legs, backed up by the huge shoulder muscles which forced his head deeper and deeper into the hairy throat of the slobbering sloth.

Now the bear tore loose from its hold, leaving a gaping wound in the sloth's throat. As the bear rolled over and over, the giant sloth toppled to the side like a great mass of quivering blubber. Blood spurted from the severed jugular vein in a crimson fountain. The little eyes closed wearily, the body shuddered convulsively, and another contest of primordial supremacy had been decided. The giant sloth was dead.

The huge bear came up on all fours, squatted to lick its wounds, and then arose on its hind legs. The sounds of the battle had attracted many other animals; they watched from a safe distance and seemed to ignore the presence of one another.

The short-faced bear glared at a pair of lionlike cats and snarled defiantly. On the other side, a pair of giant saber-tooth cats sat on their haunches, eyeing the carcass with careless indifference. In the tall grass behind the cypress tree several dire wolves watched, their red tongues slavering from their drooling jaws. A dozen yards farther back, several slinking coyotes crept into the underbrush as the bear snarled at them.

None of the lesser animals showed any real interest in the blood-drenched carcass. They had eaten well the night before and had slept soundly after the feast.

A wolf and a coyote had been trapped in the tar while trying to get at the partly submerged carcasses of the wild horses, and the body of the male saber-tooth cat had almost disappeared in the slime.

The bear roared a challenge as he faced the ring of slavering beasts, and then he began to feed on the hackberries. The lions and the saber-tooth cats moved back and crept into the tall grasses. The dire wolves had gone to their caves, leaving the carcass of the slain sloth for the natural scavengers.

Huge wings spread as the great vultures left their perches in the moss-draped trees. The Teratorni fed first, followed by the smaller condors and the large black vultures. Then came the coyotes to rend the flesh and scatter the bones, which would be polished by the rodents.

The raccoon worked back into the hole of the tree, and curled the ringed tail over his muzzle. This was life . . . and death . . . at La Brea, in the heart of old Los Angeles.

4. The Stampede

Racky stirred sluggishly as the warm rays of the afternoon sun slanted into his temporary home. He had slept soundly after the exciting adventures he had witnessed, but now he was hungry. Food there was in plenty if he could go to it, because, like the bear, Racky was omnivorous. His diet included both flesh and vegetable foods, and he could see the berries hanging on the bushes near the margin of the treacherous pool. There would also be mice and ground squirrels among the litter of bones left by the larger predators, but that could wait for the coming of night.

The wise raccoon stretched lazily and then crept forward until he was crouched at the very edge of the hole in the old dead tree. Again his nose wrinkled as a westerly wind brought the strong pungent odor of oil from the tar pits.

Racky now made further investigation of the strange phenomenon that brought death to so many and furnished food for those more fortunate. Stretching to the south and west, he could see many more of the harmless-appearing pools, which looked like water holes under the bright golden sun.

Satisfied with his discovery that there were many traps to be avoided in this new land, the raccoon turned his head to gaze out over the vast plains stretching toward the sea, and as he gazed the plains seemed to move slowly. His eyes focused for sharper vision, and he realized that the feeding grounds for the herbivores were covered by a great herd of large animals. Watching the great beasts intently, he felt more at ease, for he had seen many of them browsing in lush pastures as he had traveled south. These creatures stood seven feet high at the shoulders, because of great humps on their backs, just behind the huge shaggy heads. Short thick horns protruded from the massive skulls, and their hides were dark brown in color. These were the huge bison,[1] the ancient bovines of the Pleistocene. The bulls weighed more than a ton apiece. Unlike some of the animals that were traveling south to escape the glacial packs, the bison were migratory by nature.

Racky watched the grazing herd with desultory interest. His head raised slightly when one bull stopped grazing and sniffed the wind, which was blowing from the west. The shaggy monarch had a horn spread of more than six feet, and his glistening nostrils flared widely as he keened the breeze for some scent of warning.

The bison had poor eyesight, but few animals possessed such a sensitive sense of smell, and the watching raccoon knew that the bull bison was smelling something that Racky could now see at the fringe of trees off to the northwest—a pair of great lionlike cats watching from the coarse grass, scarcely moving, except for the tips of their long tails. As on the previous day, the big cats had placed their prey between themselves and the tar traps.

The bison monarch threw his great head back and wrinkled his nose until his upper lip curled to expose the big yellow teeth. He

---

1. *Bison antiquus* Leidy

caught the hated cat-scent to the north, the pungent smell of oil to the south, and whirled with remarkable agility to face the west, where the clean cool salt air was blowing from the ocean. A loud roar from deep in his throat brought every head erect instantly.

The bull bison dug in with his cloven hoofs, and the long shaggy hair on his head and shoulders made him seem even larger. Then he was among the cows and calves, nudging with his horns, and the herd began to race westward.

The stalking lions now threw off all pretense of stealth and bounded into the clear from the dense underbrush. The male was a magnificent brute of tremendous size, and his first leap carried him about thirty feet. The female was about a third smaller than her mate, but just as deadly and almost as fleet of foot.

The herd of bison was now in full flight, and the earth trembled with the thunder of their thudding hoofs. The bellowing of the terrified bison added to the frenzied cacophony, drowning out the usual sounds of ancient La Brea.

Some of the old cows stayed back with the half-grown calves, which could not run so fast. They had covered perhaps two hundred yards when the male lion overtook the stragglers. The lions could not hold a swift pursuit over long distances and had chosen the young bison for that reason.

A heifer calf was running beside her mother. The great male lion gathered speed and made a tremendous leap, landing heavily just behind the tender hump of the terrified heifer. As the sharp claws dug into the flesh, the young bison screamed with pain. The lion snapped viciously at the base of the neck and landed on the ground running when the heifer went down.

At the sound of the young heifer's death agony the bison bull

wheeled sharply. The herd continued in the mad stampede across the coastal plain toward the near-distant sea, but the big bull raced back to do battle with his ancient foe. The lioness was closing in on another young bison, a bull calf whose flesh would be tender and succulent. The lion was tracking the old cow who had circled to return to her slain calf.

The monarch bison came thundering up just as the huge lion shortened his stride for the leap on the old cow. The bison charged with head low, and with more than a ton of muscle and bone behind his plunging attack. The huge head struck the lion in the rump, catapulted the startled carnivore high in the air and out in front of the running cow. The lion landed on sprawling legs and did some fast footwork to regain his balance.

The bull bison was after the great cat without pausing in stride. The powerful right horn caught the staggering lion in the left side; loose skin ripped as the bison jerked his head. The wounded lion screamed with anger and pain as he tried to get to his feet. But the front shoulder was broken, and the tawny hide was red with spouting blood.

The great bull bellowed and charged again, using his tremendous head as a battering ram. The heavy skull, more than two feet wide between the horn sockets, struck the wounded lion and flattened him into a shapeless, quivering mass.

Then the bull backed away from his kill, but his triumph was short-lived. The lioness snarled soundlessly, wrinkling her lip back from the great ripping canine teeth in her powerful upper jaw, and sprang swiftly behind the bull. Her teeth flashed as she snapped at the bison's backing heels.

The bull's left leg collapsed beneath his great weight. He staggered to his feet, and again that flash of tawny hide sprang from behind. Her teeth slashed at the bull's right heel, and the bellowing monarch fell to the ground with tendons severed in both his hind legs. The lioness had hamstrung her enemy, as though to exact vengeance for the death of her mate.

With his hindquarters tucked under his muscled rump, the bull turned to face the snarling cat. The lioness faced her foe, feinted to the left, and then leaped at the bison's throat. But the long shaggy hair offered splendid protection, and the lioness barely escaped as the bull threw himself forward in an effort to crush the elusive carnivore.

Now the lioness did a strange thing. Knowing the helplessness of the bull, she snarled and went in a crouch to the slain calf. One ripping slash tore the hide and exposed the tender red flesh. She began to feed not more than twenty yards away from the bison monarch, but she had not reckoned with maternal loyalty. The old cow charged the lioness and knocked her sprawling from the carcass of the slain calf. Then the cow straddled her young, facing the infuriated lioness.

The big cat stared for a moment, her long muscular body close to the ground. The tip of her long tail twitched to tell of her anger, and her yellow eyes glared balefully as she studied the old cow.

A change came over the lioness as she backed away and circled to the right of the cow. Then the cat jumped forward, leaped to the right and to the left, and began to circle swiftly.

The bewildered cow faced about, stumbled over the body of the calf, and lunged to recover her balance. A tawny, hurtling body shot through the air with incredible speed, landed on the cow's back, and the long claws of the hind feet dug deeply into the bison's skin.

The lioness cuffed viciously with her right paw, holding on with the left. That clubbing right paw slashed three times behind the skull of the cow, and the bison moaned and went to her knees. Another cuffing blow sent her down and on her right side. Then great canine teeth sank into her throat, and another tragedy of the Pleistocene was finished.

The lioness snarled and slapped at the slain cow. Then she returned to the calf and began to feed. The coyotes gathered in a circling group to watch, drooling from slavering jaws. After the lioness had satisfied her hunger, and had taken a hindquarter for her cubs, the scavengers would close in for a feast of fresh meat.

The motionless raccoon stirred and sniffed the air. The drama had fascinated him, even though he had seen it repeated often. The hunter and the hunted, the inexorable problem of life and . . . death.

Now the lioness too was without a mate. Racky ruffled his coarse fur restlessly. Somewhere in this vast new land of wonders there must be another raccoon. Nature seldom did things by halves.

5. A New Home

The night life of La Brea was moving restlessly as the raccoon descended from his nest in the dead tree. Mice were scurrying through the grass, the nocturnal insects were humming, and the soft whir of wings meant that owls were hunting for food.

Racky skirted a small pool, not much bigger than a puddle. An acorn dropped from a live oak tree and floated on top of the water. A slithering noise warned Racky, and he crouched behind a grassy hillock. A ground squirrel[1] slid out from the grass on the other side of the little pool, reached for the floating acorn, lost its balance, and both front feet dropped into the pool.

The little squirrel tried to pull back, but that deceptive sheet of water was only an inch deep. Under the water the animal's feet were caught in the sticky black tar. A startled little bleat escaped from the frightened rodent as it tried vainly to escape.

Racky heard a swishing sound as he crouched in the dark to watch.

1. *Otospermophitus grammurus* Say

A small snake looped through the grass, its little lidless eyes focused on the trapped squirrel. The snake coiled, struck the squirrel with a swift thrust of the little flat head, and drew back.

Racky watched with a curious interest, still as a rock. He wondered how the snake would get the squirrel out from the trap; whether it could eat the furry animal, which was now partially covered with tar. The snake would swallow the squirrel whole; the powerful constrictive organs of its sinuous body would require many hours to digest the squirrel.

The waiting snake glided forward. Its jaws unhinged and opened wide to make an orifice larger than the snake's body. The snake then swallowed the squirrel's head, moved up an inch. The sharp teeth were set slanting backward to work the squirrel's body an inch farther down that capacious maw.

Racky watched with a peculiar detachment. He had found the skeletons of snakes in the woods, with the larger skeletons of toads which they had swallowed but had been unable to work down into their sinuous bodies. With food aplenty, these snakes had literally starved to death.

The snake retreated another inch and began to pull the squirrel from the viscid tar of the trap. Perhaps the snake's senses were dulled by pressure and by the excitement of the hunt. It did not hear the whirring wings of a huge horned owl[2] slanting down.

Racky, flattened out on the ground, was protected by the tall spiking bunch grass. The owl struck the snake and gripped the writhing body with its strong talons. The snake writhed convulsively, with the head and shoulders of the squirrel stuck in its throat, held inexorably by the slanting teeth which would permit passage only forward.

2. *Bubo virginianus* Gmelin

A NEW HOME

The squirrel was mired deeply in the tar, and the upward swoop of the gliding owl was terminated abruptly.

The owl was jerked down without enough room for clearance, but it refused to relax its grip. The owl struck the small pool and splattered water with its wide-spread wings. One flailing wing dipped into the tar pool, and then the hapless owl was floundering.

The forward flight of the great horned owl had carried the snake into the pool. The great bird beat the sticky tar until both wings were covered with slime, and now both feet were inescapably stuck.

Racky trembled and withdrew from his grass burrow. He knew that at any moment a skulking coyote might prowl through the brush to investigate the disturbance. The raccoon was also repulsed by the oily odor of the petroleum slime, and he remembered the sweet spring of cool clear water which was not polluted by the seepage from the subterranean oil basins.

Keeping to the shelter of the high coarse grass, the raccoon moved stealthily toward the small stream which flowed south and west to the sea. Many of the herbivores watered in the flowing creek; such animals as the horses and bison. Their sharp hoofs had torn up the ground in the softer places, exposing the roots of succulent grasses and small bushes.

Racky ate a salad course to ease the gnawing hunger in his belly. He washed each bit of root carefully in the water before eating, meanwhile keeping his ears tuned for any sound which would warn him of approaching danger. He had seen the hawks and eagles circling in the blue sky; the long-billed storks and herons, and the repulsive condors and vultures. All lived off the land, had remarkable eyesight, and were always hungry. The great horned owls and lesser raptors, which were nocturnal like himself, could see better in the dark than in the light of day, and Racky remembered the swift attack of the great horned owl at the small tar pool.

A small juniper tree[3] grew on the south bank of the little stream, its branches stretching to the north bank. The raccoon climbed the tree and crossed on a low branch, but he crouched for a moment before lowering himself to the ground, for he had noticed the habits of the animals, and he always remembered what he had seen. The horses and bison were grass-eating mammals, and unless water was abundant near their feeding grounds, they always sought the water holes in the early morning, or just before sunset. The ferocious carnivores, such as the lions and wolves, came to slake their thirst after night had closed down. That is, unless they stalked the water holes in search of food . . . while the herbivores were drinking.

Racky heard a lapping noise, and he saw a shaggy brown creature silhouetted against the dark sky toward the north. The raccoon settled to rest, and to watch. The strange creature was much like the giant sloth which had been slain by the short-faced bear, except that it was much smaller. It was as large as the lionlike cat, much heavier in bulk, and moved very slowly.

Racky recognized the beast; this was the small ground sloth,[4] much like its larger relative. It had the same powerful tail and pillarlike hind legs. The forelegs were longer than those of the giant sloth, in proportion to their respective sizes, and these legs terminated in strong, digging claws.

The ground sloth moved forward toward a clump of yucca,[5] walking on the sides of its feet. It grunted softly as it reached for the yucca,

3. *Juniperus californica* Carr
4. *Northrotherium shastense* Sinclair
5. *Yuca gloriosa*

after which the beast sat up on its hind legs, using the thick tail for a brace.

Racky could hear the grinding teeth chewing up the succulent leaves of the yucca. The body of the huge animal was like a black shadow against the gray of the skyline. Racky's keen eyes narrowed as he saw something move, over on the distant horizon.

Several dark shapes were coming toward the stream in a crouching advance, with shoulders high and heads held low—the powerful dire wolves which sometimes hunted in packs. Racky knew the ways of these scavengers. They had evidently been unsuccessful at finding food, and desperately hungry, they would attack even a sloth. The sloth was most often immune from the large predators because of the strong taint of its flesh.

The stupid sloth continued to eat, and the huge wolves drew ever closer. They were like wraiths of the night as they crossed the plains, crouching low to the ground.

Racky flattened out on the limb of the juniper, and he seemed almost a part of the tree. He could see the pack of wolves spreading out in a semicircle behind the sluggish sloth. One huge wolf crouched a trifle ahead of the pack bellied low to the ground, with out-thrust head almost touching the earth. A savage snarl ripped from the leader's throat as the big male wolf sprang at the sloth, with slashing teeth ripping at the thick loose hide.

Only then did the sloth stop feeding. It growled and turned slowly to face the snarling pack, forming a tripod with its hind legs and thick tail. The sloth held its front legs in front of its enormous belly and chest.

The wolves rushed in, leaped to right and left, and forced the sloth down by superior weight in numbers. The odor of fresh blood tainted the night air and drove the wolf pack mad with hunger. The big leader ripped at the soft belly of the sloth. He was followed by several other wolves, which slashed and leaped away. Then the pack withdrew and sat on their haunches facing their helpless prey, keeping the death watch.

The sloth foundered helplessly, wounded grievously in a score of places. That last terrible attack had been directed against its vitals, and finally it stopped slobbering and shuddered convulsively. The male wolf sniffed the air, barked shortly, and the pack sprang to the feast. Knowing that the coyotes would not be far away, the raccoon crept back across the low branch of the tree.

When the wolves were almost hidden in the cavern of the sloth's belly, Racky lowered himself to the ground and made his stealthy way to the east, keeping under cover of the tall bunch grass. When he was a safe distance from the wolf pack he climbed a low tree and looked back. He could now see another crouching circle of moving shapes against the skyline; these would be the coyotes, which would devour what the wolves left.

Racky flattened out and watched the ground beneath his perch. A tiny creature hopped from behind a clump of grass, and the raccoon dropped like a plummet. His left hand closed around a kangaroo rat,[6] and Racky had his meat course for the evening meal.

When the small animal had stopped struggling, the raccoon carried it to the stream, tore the skin from the flesh, and washed the meat with meticulous care. After finishing his meal, the raccoon washed his hands in the cold water, slaked his thirst, and started on his quest for more desirable quarters.

He crossed the stream on the branch of a cypress tree, dropped to the ground where cover was plentiful, and headed north and west.

6. *Dipodomys agilis* Gambel

A NEW HOME

The prevailing wind was from the west to the east, and just before daybreak Racky came to a group of large live oak trees[7] on a small knoll far removed from the tar traps.

He chose a hoary old monarch in the center of the group, climbed the trunk nimbly, and sighed with satisfaction. His conjecture had been accurate. High above the ground in the main trunk of the giant oak, there was a large hole. After making sure that there were no snakes in his new home, Racky settled himself in a ball and curled the black-and-white tail up over his muzzle.

Now the odors of La Brea did not annoy the sagacious raccoon, but he stirred restlessly. The new home was large enough for two. . . .

---

7. *Quercus agrifolia* Nee

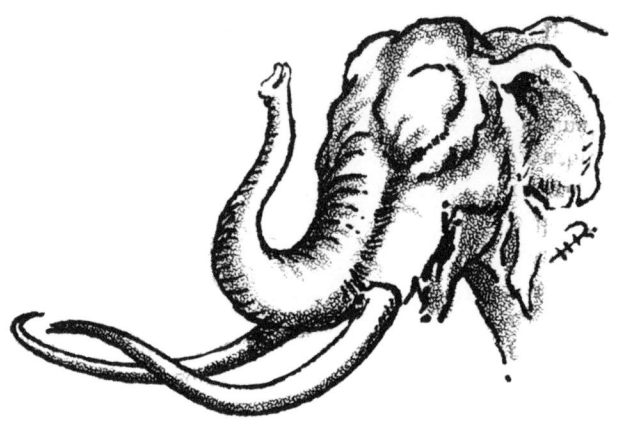

6. Life at La Brea

The long shadows of twilight were lengthening when the astute raccoon crept to the front of his new home. He sniffed the west wind inquiringly and filled his lungs with the clean sweet air from the sea. Then he settled down to study the surroundings of his newly acquired home.

Now he was to the west of the tar pits, which he could see in the distance. The red rays of a dying sun made the treacherous pools shimmer with ever-changing colors. Distance always lends enchantment. Racky's eyes widened with interest.

Something new had been added to the largest pool while the raccoon had slept. He could see what seemed to be a small island in the lake, and then the island moved sluggishly. A faint trumpeting came to the raccoon's keen ears, and he saw a part of the dark blotch detach itself and then wave frantically in the air. The sun was reflected from a pair of long white tusks, and the raccoon recognized the newly entrapped animal.[1] He had seen several of the huge beasts in the forests to the north, stripping leaves from the lower branches of trees with their long tenuous trunks.

---

1. *Mastodon americanus* Kerr

Racky watched curiously as the huge elephant tried to free its feet from the tar trap. On the edge of the lake, between the raccoon and the helpless mastodon, many of the animals of La Brea had gathered to watch the losing and unequal struggle against death. A pair of saber-tooth cats crouched under a huge cypress, and, in the scaly branches above, several Teratorni preened their plumage with curved beaks. Off to one side, a savage pair of dire wolves sat on their haunches, their heads out-thrust in that peculiar position which made them always seem to be pulling some heavy weight. But here was something they could not move; the mastodon weighed at least five tons. The ever-present coyotes were slinking in the background. The great lionlike cats were absent; perhaps they knew the futility of attempting to reach the struggling pachyderm. Only the condors and vultures would feast before the weight of the beast sank beneath the iridescent surface of the lake. The bones would be perfectly preserved in the asphalt, down through the ages.

Racky turned his eyes away from the trapped beast. He was thankful that he had moved from the dead tree above the treacherous trap. He could no longer smell the pungent tar or the desiccating flesh of animals enmired beyond the reach of the scavengers. He raised his head to observe the flight of a hunting falcon,[2] which was circling high above the trees. The hawk zoomed down in pursuit of a band-tailed pigeon,[3] struck the smaller bird in flight, and caught the falling body with its strong talons. Then a duck hawk[4] floated on outspread pinions above the water holes, and it made a power dive at a black-bellied plover[5] swimming on the surface of a fresh-water creek.

2. *Falco mexicanus* Schlegel
3. *Zenaidura macroura* Linnaeus
4. *Falcro peregrinus* Tunstall
5. *Squatarola squatarola* Linnaeus

Racky watched the great birds at their hunting and waited for the coming of darkness. As the shadows lengthened he could hear the sleepy call of quail[6] as they sought their nests in low bushes near the cluster of live oak trees.

Racky leaned forward when a small bird streaked across a little clearing, running with queer long-legged strides. The head was carried low and well forward on a long neck. This was the caracara,[7] which fed on carrion, and the wise raccoon knew that an animal had been slain in the immediate vicinity. Racky's nose curled disdainfully. He was no scavenger unless forced by necessity to take the leavings of the carnivores. His eyes glowed in the gloom as he thought of the quail in the nearby thicket. Perhaps there would be eggs in the nests. He had also marked a likely place in the little creek where crayfish might be found under the flat rocks.

Far out on the coastal plains horses and bison were grazing quietly, but Racky could see the sentinels on guard for sight or scent of danger. A pair of giant sloths were feeding on yucca near the flowing stream, trusting to their size and unpalatable flesh for a partial immunity.

The twilight deepened and gave way to the encroaching shades of night. The night insects were beginning their incessant hum of sound, interrupted occasionally by the cries of owls, which circled above the foliage in search of food.

Racky crept from the hole in the tree, lowered himself down the scaly bark to the ground, and scuttled into a patch of undergrowth. His eyes glowed as he found a faint trail under the low bushes. He was now the hunter, and the pangs of hunger sharpened his senses. With ears tuned to catch the slightest sound, he stealthily followed the trail

---

6. *Lophortyx californica* Shaw
7. *Polyborus prelutosus* Howard

made by the quail. His nostrils flared widely at the sound of a soft cheeping call, and as he turned slightly toward the sound, he flattened out in a crouch. He could see a collection of twigs and grass, hidden cunningly in a cluster of rocks and protected by the taller bunch grass.

Racky began to move slowly toward the hidden nest, but just before he reached it, the hen quail left the nest and flew to a low bush. Racky went right to the nest and smelled curiously. Then he reached in with his left paw, which was much like a hand, picked up an egg, and broke it on the ground. There were three eggs in the nest, but only a heap of broken shells was left when Racky again took up the hunt.

He kept to the bunch grass for concealment as he made his way toward the creek. Several times, when owls swooped low in pursuit of mice, he sought the shelter of rocks, and once he took to a tree when he saw the skulking form of a prowling coyote following his trail.

It was nearing midnight when Racky reached the creek and crept up the trunk of a stunted juniper tree to scout the immediate vicinity. He saw the coyote leap after a frightened hare, and not until he was satisfied that the coast was clear did the raccoon lower himself to the ground and approach some flat rocks which provided a crossing at the little stream. There he squatted and turned over a flat stone. A crayfish[8] backed hurriedly away, but the raccoon caught it dexterously.

After catching several of the tasty crustaceans, Racky moved away from the stream and turned up a flat dry rock. A black stinkbug[9] stood on its head, and the raccoon had it in his grasp. Another rock yielded a terrified pocket mouse,[10] and added to the variety of the raccoon's diet.

Racky satisfied his thirst, lapping the cool water noisily. Then, as though aware of his lack of caution, he scuttled to a low-growing tree

8. *Cambarus affinis*
9. *Eleodes*
10. *Perognathus californicus* Merriam

and quickly climbed up to an overhanging limb. For several minutes he remained motionless. The sickle moon was high in the sky, a cool wind was blowing from the ocean, and the hunting had been successful.

Even the low-flying owls and other night birds zoomed overhead with less frequency. Out on the vast plains the horses and bison were grazing quietly. The crouching raccoon placed all the night noises accurately, and he was about to descend from the tree when a slight breeze caused him to raise his head and sniff cautiously.

Eyes and ears were not enough to guarantee safety in the wild land of the Pleistocene era. Most often a warning would come through the sense of smell. Racky's nose wrinkled with distaste when the odor of a male coyote came down the wind, and he knew that the beast was not far away. As he turned to face the new danger the ruff of coarse hair bristled up behind his head. His lips snarled back soundlessly to show strong white teeth set firmly in heavy capable jaws. He would avoid conflict if it were possible to retreat, but he would fight viciously if cornered.

Now the hated scent of the coyote was more pronounced, and Racky crouched on the large branch in silent watchfulness. Perhaps a hundred yards toward the west, Racky saw a dark shadow move swiftly from a brushy covert. A large coyote crossed an open clearing in a patch of pale moonlight, with head low to the grounds, as though following a fresh trail.

Racky narrowed his eyes as he watched the skulking scavenger. He was not disturbed about his own trail, which had long since grown cold. He could take to a taller tree if pursued, but he was vaguely worried by the presence of the coyote. He settled down to wait for the coyote to leave the vicinity, wondering why the hunting animal was alone. They usually traveled in pairs or with the pack. Doubtless there was meat aplenty nearer the tar pits, and Racky thought of the hapless mastodon trapped in the lake.

Back and forth through the shadows and moonlight, the skulking coyote quartered and searched. A fleet-footed hare bounded out of the brush and hopped rapidly across the clearing. The coyote whirled about, but after one glance at the fleeing hare turned back to the shadows and resumed his search.

Racky watched with wrinkles furrowing his brow. Ordinarily the coyote would have raced after the hare, and these actions were puzzling.

The coyote was moving closer to Racky's hiding place, and every hair stiffened on the raccoon's back. He stifled a low snarling growl deep in his throat, and he relaxed somewhat when the coyote quartered to the west. For some reason unknown to the raccoon, the cowardly coyote was not following the regular pattern. The coyote had found a hot scent, but the quarry eluded him.

The answer came to Racky when the wind changed slightly and blew directly toward him from the west. He detected a new odor above the rancid smell of the coyote, and a change swept over the usually placid raccoon.

He had made a diligent search in all the likely places, but his efforts had gone unrewarded. Now he knew that his long quest was at an end, but perhaps it was . . . too late.

7. Ricky Arrives

Racky felt a surge of excitement in every healthy muscle of his strong body. In his eagerness, he almost forgot his native caution, and then he restrained the leap that would have carried him to the ground. Again he quivered as the west wind bore an unmistakable message to his sensitive nostrils. One of his own kind was out there in the rubble and underbrush, and that other raccoon was a female. Racky was as sure of this fact as he was that the female raccoon was in deadly peril. He knew now why the wily coyote was circling, and the raccoon's lips skinned back to show tightly clenched teeth.

Racky also knew that the female raccoon was a stranger to La Brea. He remembered his own feeling of insecurity during those first few days after he had reached this place in the south land. He trembled with eagerness and with fear, but there was nothing he could do but watch . . . and wait.

The coyote was closer now, not more than fifty yards away. The large beast was stalking stiff-legged toward a pile of volcanic rock almost hidden by the tall coarse grass. Then, in a language he could understand, Racky heard a shrill frantic plea for help. The female raccoon knew of her dire peril, and she was also aware that Racky was close by. Now the astute raccoon knew that the female had been trying to follow his wandering trail. He climbed up on an overhanging branch and called inquiringly.

An answer came instantly from the rubble of rocks—a low wavering call, ending on a high note of urgency. This was the mating call, and a change transformed the crouching raccoon. He was now the dominant male who had found his mate.

He trembled with anger as he watched the skulking coyote stalk closer to the quarry that had been trailed for so long. Then anger gave way to cunning, and he showed why none of his kind had ever been trapped in the tar pits, for nature had provided him with brains.

Racky leaped to the ground, plainly visible in the silvery moonlight. An arrogant challenge blasted from his snarling lips as he stalked stiff-legged in full view of the coyote. Then he stiffened his back and, crouching low to the ground, moved toward the surprised coyote. As he advanced toward his much larger adversary, Racky was remembering every bit of the terrain and cover in the immediate vicinity.

With the ruff bristling behind his head to form a collar, Racky snarled at the coyote as he continued his advance. He was a distant relative of the great short-faced bear, and of the smaller grizzly.[1] He had searched vainly for one of his own kind, and now that he had found a mate he would either take her to his home or die while trying.

The coyote came out of a crouch and whirled to face the snarling raccoon coming toward him. A savage growl curled back the scavenger's lips; then he recovered from his surprise and rushed to meet the challenging raccoon.

1. *Ursus horribilis* Ord

Racky bellied low to the ground and barked sharply. Talking in his own language, he told the female to seek safety in flight, and also not to worry about him, but to find refuge in the tree he had so lately vacated.

The savage coyote was now coming swiftly, depending on his size and strength to overwhelm this impudent upstart who had dared to challenge him. His lips snarled back to show the great ripping teeth, set in powerful jaws that could crush a large bone.

Racky veered suddenly to the left, straightened out, and then darted to the right. The coyote broke stride and dissipated some of the fury of his charge. Racky rose up and snarled insults at the leaping wild dog bearing down upon him. The coyote was only yards away and coming in fast. The raccoon took a little leap forward, and suddenly darted to the side, rolling over and over in a muscular ball. He rolled right under the charging coyote's front legs, tripping that surprised bully before the coyote could check his forward rush. As the coyote went down in a tripping fall, Racky came to his feet and streaked across the clearing with unsuspected speed.

The coyote yelped with anger and stopped his tumbling fall. When he came to his feet he whirled swiftly and took up the pursuit.

The raccoon was now back to the tree he had left, and he went up the scaly bark like a streak of dull gray light. Snapping teeth just missed the raccoon's hind legs, and the hot fetid odor of the scavenger's breath fanned the ruff on Racky's neck.

Racky heard the thud of feet as the coyote fell back to the ground at the foot of the tree. But now the cunning raccoon had reached the overhanging branch. He turned instantly to face the coyote, who was barking furiously under the tree, and Racky crept to the very edge and watched the frustrated canine.

Racky flattened out on the branch, peering down with eyes that held the wisdom of the ages. His was the highest intelligence quotient of all his contemporaries of the Pleistocene era, and he had proved his right to survival.

Racky did not move when he felt a slight vibration of the branch behind him. Although the danger had passed momentarily, he knew that the echoing shrieks of the disappointed coyote would bring other scavengers.

The coyote sat on his haunches at the foot of the tree, howling shrilly to tell that he had treed a quarry. The long red tongue slavered hungrily from the cruel drooling jaws, and other scavengers were giving tongue as they sped in for the kill.

Racky's hair stiffened when something touched his flank. He turned his head and sniffed slowly, and a feeling of partial content came to him as he tested the scent of his own kind. Somewhere in this vast new land there had been another raccoon, and his own had come to him at last.

Racky quivered as a warm plump body pressed close to his own, and a moist muzzle sniffed at the back of his neck and at his pointed ears. He turned his head and acknowledged the caress, and then he again gave his attention to the howling coyote.

The female raccoon pressed close to him, and he could feel the terror that caused her body to tremble. Racky grunted, but he curved his body to give the female more room. There would be time for getting acquainted later, when the danger of snapping jaws had passed.

Swift loping shapes appeared on the skyline and bore in to join the yapping coyote at the foot of the tree. Now there was a half-ring of menacing coyotes surrounding the tree, and only the brawling creek prevented the scavengers from completing the circle.

Racky snarled provocatively. While the assailants could not climb the tree, it was also true that Racky and his mate could not leave their precarious shelter.

As the yapping chorus rose in volume and intensity, the female raccoon crept closer to Racky, and her trembling increased. Racky gave way a trifle more, and his head went over that of the female in a protective gesture. His tongue licked out and smoothed the hair behind her flattened ears, and gradually the female relaxed and did not tremble so violently.

Racky began to talk in little barking grunts. He was telling his companion that he had found a fine new home, and that he was no Johnny-come-lately to the hunting grounds of La Brea.

The perfume of her body soothed him, but Racky maintained a watchful vigil. The coyotes threw back their heads and howled ravenously, and Racky shuddered as he thought of the larger and more powerful dire wolves which might be attracted by that echoing chorus. It was true that if the dire wolves came they would scatter the cowardly coyotes like leaves before a strong wind. But then they would take the places of the coyotes.

He raised his head and scanned the skyline intently, narrowing his eyes to shed the waning light of the fading sickle moon. His fears were realized when he saw two crouching shapes silhouetted against the sky, huge doglike creatures holding their heads low and forward as though they were pulling at a heavy burden.

The female also saw the newcomers, and once more she began to tremble. Racky turned his head and licked her face reassuringly. Then the dire wolves saw the circle of coyotes and came leaping to the attack.

So intent were the coyotes that they failed to see or hear the wolves until the male wolf was among them with snapping teeth. The big male coyote yelped as the bones were broken in one of his front legs, and as he was limping away another coyote went down with throat torn open.

The smaller female wolf also accounted for a coyote before the pack took to their heels in terrorized flight. The huge male wolf lunged at the coyote the female had crippled, snapped just once, and threw the lifeless body of the coyote over a huge shoulder, where it splashed into the brawling creek.

Racky watched with every hair on his body standing erect. He could feel the female trembling violently beside him, and she whimpered when the male wolf leaped at the stunted tree. When she saw that the wolf had failed to reach their perch by a good six feet, the female settled down in a crouch, pressing close to Racky for what comfort she could find.

Racky knew of the patience of the dire wolves. They would keep their vigil for days and nights, until hunger or weakness forced their prey to attempt an escape. One of them would remain on guard while the other foraged for food, and they could deny water to the raccoons, while having a plentiful supply at their very feet.

It is a law of nature that all creatures of the wild can recognize their own kind by smell; even when they cannot see the animal they know it is close by or has passed that way.

Racky raised his head and keened the westerly wind from force of long habit. A tremor ran through his wiry muscular body, and he sniffed deeply again to verify his discovery. The female was also testing the wind, and Racky knew that she had smelled their distant relative when she half-rose from a crouch.

Now Racky was certain that the great short-faced bear was coming toward them from the west. There was no mistaking that strong musky odor of *Tremarctotherium simum,* the strongest and fiercest animal of the Pleistocene era.

There is no way of knowing whether Racky knew that blood was thicker than water, but he was a relative to the short-faced bear, and it was worth a try. The raccoon raised his head and shrilled a loud cry of distress. He repeated the call when an answering roar came from the near distance.

Racky peered down at the menacing wolves, and he knew that they also had caught the scent of the dreaded bear. They growled savagely with heads together, and then turned slightly toward the west.

Racky was watching the horizon, and he was the first to see a giant head top the rise as the huge bear stood erect on powerful hind legs. Once more he gave a bleating call, and the great bear dropped to all fours and came toward the creek at a lumbering gallop.

The dire wolves cringed back, took one good look, and fled precipitously. And as they raced into the shadows, Racky nudged the female raccoon with an urgent shoulder. He chattered in a whisper as he crawled past her and dropped to the ground on the opposite side of the creek.

The great bear had saved them from a long imprisonment, and perhaps from a worse fate. But the short-faced bear could also climb a tree if he so desired, and, after all, their relationship was distant and a more or less tenuous matter.

With the female at his shoulder Racky raced through the underbrush, taking to the creek occasionally to wipe out the scent of their tracks. Across the plains they ran, keeping to the high bunch grass and volcanic rock, until they came at last to the grove of live oak trees where Racky had taken up his new home.

He streaked up the big tree, the female at his heels. With his usual native caution, Racky paused at the entrance to his home to make sure no intruder had pre-empted those quarters during his absence. Then he crawled quickly inside, calling softly to his mate to follow him. He curled his muzzle over her neck and settled down for a good long talk, and what he said to her was between himself and Ricky. That was his name for his mate, and now his faith was justified. Somewhere in this wild new land he had found another raccoon. His own had come to him.

8. Ricky and Racky

Life at La Brea assumed a new aspect for the happily mated raccoons. They no longer walked alone or fretted with the uneasiness of the lonely. A week had passed since that night of terror when Racky had offered himself as bait to the savage coyote so that Ricky might escape and find safety in the tree by the brawling creek—a week of getting acquainted while the happy pair were on their honeymoon.

Racky had taken Ricky to the tar pits so that she might see the daily tragedies and be warned thereby. He knew all the nesting places of the quail, the haunts of the delicious crayfish, and where the timid field mice could be found. They feasted on hackberries, and on the blue elderberries[1] that grew in abundance by flowing springs.

There had been long lazy days in the roomy quarters high up in the live oak tree, to which Ricky had now added the feminine touch. She told Racky of the perils of her long migration from the north, of the strange animals she had seen, and of her many narrow escapes from death. This was an old story to Racky, who had experienced the same trying ordeals. He nodded wisely, showed the proper interest, and expressed his contentment with his new estate.

1. *Sambucus glauca* Nutt

During the long warm hours of twilight, before they began their nocturnal hunting, Racky told Ricky of the habits of the animals and birds which made up the La Brea assemblage. He illustrated his talks with visual proofs, showing her the saber-tooth cats, the great lionlike cats, and the massive giant sloths. These were nearly always present near the tar traps, and Ricky was properly impressed. Like her mate, that which she had seen once she would always remember.

Ricky had learned something of the pattern of life at La Brea. She had become familiar with the feeding habits of the great carnivores, the grass-eating animals such as horses and bison, the skulking scavengers such as the dire wolves and the coyotes, and the huge birds that haunted the pools. She had also learned the locations of trees that could provide refuge during their nightly hunting expeditions, in the event that they were themselves hunted by the predatory coyotes.

Now the two raccoons were safely perched in the hole of the old dead tree above the lake, the largest of the pools. Racky rested against the bark where he could watch the changing scene below. Ricky was curled up just behind her mate, her head resting on his shoulder, her muzzle between his pointed ears.

At such times as these audible articulation was unnecessary. Ricky could tell by the sudden tensing of Racky's muscles when something unusual had attracted his attention. She could follow the direction of his head and of his wise sharp eyes. During times like these, theirs was the companionship of silence, when each could indicate by a slight pressure, and the other would understand.

Ricky felt the muscles move suddenly in Racky's back as he tensed and slightly raised his head. She followed the direction of his inquisitive ears, and they both poised tensely to watch a dark moving shape in the hackberry thicket near the edge of the pool.

Racky's nostrils were sniffing, and both raccoons recognized the odor that sifted along the edge of the westerly wind, above the pungent smell of the always-present oil. The creature in the thicket made plenty of noise, but they knew that it was not the great short-faced bear.

As they watched, they saw a pair of saber-tooth cats take positions near the thicket, crouched on the ground in the underbrush. On the west side of the berry patch a pair of lionlike cats sat on their haunches to watch. Under the cypress tree in which the Teratorni roosted they could see a pair of dire wolves, while farther back in the brush were the cowardly coyotes.

Even the great condor-like birds stirred sluggishly, and Ricky could hear them shifting to get better purchase with their talons on the large branches.

The bushes were waving as the animal gathered in the luscious fruit, and then the watching raccoons saw him move into the clear. Racky stared at the black bear,[2] for which the watching animals showed a marked respect. Although not so large as his cousin, the short-faced bear, the newcomer was a huge beast with a small head and short powerful jaws armed with huge grinding teeth.

The feeding bear seemed oblivious to the animals in the background. The raccoons could hear his grunts of satisfaction as he shoveled in the hackberries. When he had satisfied his hunger, the black bear roared an invitation.

Ricky crept closer to Racky when a smaller bear crashed through the growth to join her mate. The male bear stood guard while the female fed, and when she took a step toward the edge of the pool he growled a savage warning. The female returned obediently to her feed-

2. *Ursus optimus* Schultz

ing, and when she had satisfied her hunger she followed her lord and master, who led a crashing advance through the underbrush.

The lionlike cats and the saber-tooth cats gave way before that bold exit, and the coyotes fled for cover. The huge dire wolves crept behind the tall tough grass under the trees until the black bears had left the vicinity of the pools.

Racky knew that the male bear was leading the way to a spring of fresh water. He raised his head with an inquiring sniff when an unfamiliar odor drifted down the westerly wind. Ricky was sitting up behind him, sniffing the wind as a questioning expression wrinkled her face. She nudged Racky suggestively, but received no explanation. Racky was staring intently at an aisle between the trees, and his eyes narrowed slightly when a strange apparition took form and came toward the pools from the northwest.

Only the great vultures could be seen in their trees against the skyline. The predatory carnivores were evidently lurking in hidden coverts beside the trail, and they too were evidently puzzled by this strange creature that was coming toward the lake.

Racky settled down to watch, and then a second creature followed the first. The two strangers were larger than horses or bison, and their huge splatted feet padded softly through the grass. They were long-legged, had short tails and long slender necks which supported proportionately small heads. There was a small hump well forward on each broad back. This was the two raccoons' first look at a migratory camel.[3]

The beasts were perhaps eight feet tall, and they moved slowly with measured tread. They were now nearing the drooping cypress tree, and Racky wrinkled his nose when he caught the strong odor of

3. *Camelops hesternus* Leidy

tainted breath. Evidently the camels were thirsty, and had not smelled the clean water of the creek because of the cross-wind which was blowing from the southwest.

Racky's spine stiffened slightly as he raised a trifle and leaned forward. He had seen the slight movement of the brush under the trees, but the large male camel had evidently not detected the agitation.

Death was lurking there by the lake of petroleum tar, but the unsuspecting camels were intent only on slaking their thirst. The slightly smaller female camel swayed after her mate, walking in his tracks.

Ricky lay tensely behind her spouse, watching the drama unfold below their hiding place. Again she felt that strange tingle of terror, and she could feel the tenseness of Racky's sturdy body.

A half-moon cast a silvery glow across La Brea. The night insects were humming their nocturnal songs, broken only by the soft padding soles of the huge feet which were set behind the two large toes.

The eerie stillness of the night was shattered suddenly by a screaming roar. A great male lion leaped high into the air and landed on the back of the male camel. The female lion leaped at the smaller camel, and the huge beasts squalled with fright as great claws sank deeply into their hides.

The male lion slapped viciously with his right paw, and the camel went to his knees under the blow. Another clubbing smash sent the male camel sprawling to the ground, where he coughed and moaned. His neck was broken.

The lioness was having more trouble with her victim. Lacking the striking power of her mate, she clubbed the female camel with repeated blows before the stricken beast went to her knees. The lioness lunged forward and sank her teeth into the long neck at the base of the spine, and she leaped to the ground as the camel went down at the very margin of the deceptive pool. Now the male lion rushed at his prey and severed the jugular vein. Both lions started to feed on the kill.

Racky glanced into the brush behind the trees. He frowned when he observed no familiar lurking scavengers, but he knew the reason when the wind changed. The musky odor of bear was unmistakable. Ricky followed the direction of Racky's pointing ears. She shuddered slightly when she saw a pair of short-faced bears coming down the trail through the trees.

Racky knew that while the bears could not catch their more fleet-footed contemporaries in pursuit, the bears were also robbers. They were more than a match for even the great lionlike cats.

The male lion raised his head suddenly and sniffed the wind. A low growl welled up in his throat, and the lioness stopped feeding to watch her mate. The lion was staring up the trail, and only the tip of his long tail twitched nervously to tell of his anger. Then the lion recognized the great bears and growled a warning to his mate.

The two lions slunk into the brush without making a challenge. The two bears rushed up to the camels, their awkward ambling advance belying their speed.

The big male reached the carcasses first and ripped the hide well back from the hump of the large camel. Then the bear tore out a chunk of shoulder meat and chewed slowly. He grunted with disgust and turned to watch his mate, who was also chewing slowly. After her second bite her lips curled above her huge teeth and she threw her head back with a snarl of distaste.

The male bear grunted and ambled away through the trees on all fours, followed by its mate. The unsavory meat of the slain camels was left to the scavengers, and Racky twitched when the coyotes and wolves began to appear.

Now was a good time for him and Ricky to make an exit. There would be crayfish under the rocks bordering the creek, quail eggs for the taking closer to home ... and safety.

The cautious raccoons climbed down the dead tree, one on each side, merged with the protective underbrush, and scurried along to hunting grounds more suited to their tastes.

They could hear the excited yapping of the coyotes, the growls of the dire wolves, and the stirring of wings from the vultures above the pools.

Ricky kept close to Racky as they sought the game trails well back from the traps of death. They came to the brawling creek and turned over several flat stones. When they caught crayfish, they removed the shells and washed the firm white meat in the cold water before breaking their fasts.

Another day and night had sifted into the infinity of uncounted years, leaving an indelible record in the death traps of old La Brea.

9. The Rains Come

A gentle rain was falling when Racky crept to the front of his home high in the live oak tree. The raccoon chattered the news over his shoulder to Ricky, who was tidying up the living room and making herself presentable. Ricky came to join her spouse for a moment, to watch the crystal-clear water drip from the sharp-pointed leaves of their arboreal bungalow.

It was late afternoon, and the grass-eaters were drinking in the creek which flowed through the grazing grounds of the broad coastal plains. The wild horses and bison were numerous, and a pair of the tall camels were lazily chewing their cuds as they stood close to a bosque of trees near the little stream.

Farther away, Racky could see a pair of giant sloths feeding on succulent leaves of yucca plants. There were also several of the smaller sloths, while farther back in the underbrush a dozen coyotes were watching from cover.

Racky showed interest when several wading birds alighted on the stream and began to fish with their long beaks. Storks were plentiful, with here and there a snowy egret[1] fluffing its beautiful feathers against the gentle rain. One peculiar swanlike bird[2] raised its head and whistled musically at its mate. In a covert of tules Racky could see the slender wiry body of a gray fox.

The fox was watching the whistling swan, keeping his pointed nose well down. The fox had taken a position on the south bank where the wind from the west would not betray his presence.

Racky watched the whistling swan wade ever closer to the margin of the stream, searching for tiny fish which sought refuge close to the roots of the tules. The swan would dart its head down and spear swiftly with its bill, unmindful of the danger lurking in the swamp grass.

Several mallard ducks[3] were feeding close to the north bank of the creek, quacking with quiet content. Racky saw a speck in the sky; it grew larger as it approached the feeding grounds of the water fowl. It was a duck hawk. High in the air over the creek it hovered, poised for a moment, and then made a swooping dive.

The whistling swan was the first to see the lancing shadow, and it whistled shrilly and flapped for a take-off. As the mallard arose from the stream, the duck hawk struck swiftly, sinking its talons into the duck. The hawk swooped up, its powerful wings flailing under the burden.

Racky stiffened and leaned forward to watch with narrowed eyes.

1. *Egretta thula* Molina
2. *Cygnus columbianus* Ord
3. *Anas platyrhynchos* Linnaeus

He saw the whistling swan clear the water at the very edge of the stream where the gray fox was waiting. The fox leaped high with jaws snapping, caught the swan by one leg, and dragged it down.

All the birds were now awing, giving their various cries of alarm and fright. The gray fox dragged the swan away from the creek, leaped upon it and broke the curving neck, and then dragged the bird back into the tules where it could eat without too much danger from coyotes.

The giant sloths did not look up from their feeding. The pair of camels chewed their cuds, belching occasionally with lazy eyes half closed. The horses and bison grazed on the bunch grass, depending on their leaders who stood guard against surprise.

Racky watched and stirred restlessly. He was thinking of the crayfish and mud turtles,[4] of the quail eggs, while waiting for the coming of darkness.

The wild horses were moving toward the west, where the open plains would provide better protection against attack by the lionlike cats. The mares neighed shrilly to call half-grown colts that showed a tendency to wander away.

The shades of twilight fell over the land, and the drizzling rain brought a leaden haze which lessened visibility. Far over to the northwest Racky saw several menacing shapes take form at the edge of a bison wallow. The dire wolves, easily distinguishable by the forward thrust of their heads, were gathering in a pack. With the cunning of their kind, they had kept to the windward of the grazing horse band. They were now out of sight, but Racky knew that the pack had gathered in the deep depression to avoid detection.

A huge stallion turned and keened the wind with his head held high and nostrils flaring wide. His massive chest was criss-crossed

---

4. *Clemmys*

with the scars of many a battle. His sharp hoofs gave mute evidence of the fight he could wage. He turned again to the band and watched the mares jealously, and a shrill neigh urged the band to accelerate the pace.

Ricky crept up behind Racky and settled down with her head on his shoulder. The gentle rain continued to fall, giving promise of abundant feed and a replenishment of the water courses. The rain would also add danger to the deceptive oil pools, and many an unwary animal would be trapped when it went to drink.

Racky, staring intently at the bison wallow, saw a head raise slowly in the murky gloom. The time was that indeterminate period between sunset and night, when the tricky half-light created optical illusions. Shadows seemed tremendous in size; an object would appear closer at hand, or farther away.

The horse band was a short distance north of the wallow when Racky saw the first huge wolf outlined against the leaden sky. Several other heads appeared, until they numbered a score or more. The heads were followed by lean crouching bodies as the pack of dire wolves made ready for the attack, after first making sure that the great stallion was at the head of the horse band.

One huge wolf seemed to be the leader. He kept well in advance of his companions as they stalked the old mares with colts, which were the stragglers of the herd. The wolves moved forward, bellied down low to the ground, using the thick bunch grass for concealment. Racky watched, with Ricky pressing close to him, as the wolf pack approached ever closer to the unsuspecting horses. The two raccoons were tense, knowing what would happen when the great wolf gave the signal for the attack.

The leader now stretched from his crouch, gathering his muscular flanks beneath him for a running start. Then he was away with the speed of hunger. He flashed under a yearling colt and slashed at the tender unprotected throat. The other wolves were now among the startled horses, ripping and snarling as they caught the scent of fresh blood.

The big stallion whirled and raced back when the first scream of agony burst from the throat of the yearling colt. The old mares were kicking savagely at the marauders and waging a losing fight.

The main body of the horse herd took refuge in swift flight, but most of the old mares refused to leave their screaming colts. The stallion charged in with great teeth snapping, front feet clawing, and his heels kicking viciously. His first target was the wolf leader, who was starting to feed on the yearling colt. The stallion struck down with his front hoofs, hitting the wolf just behind the head. As the wolf went down and rolled over, the stallion reared high and came down with chopping front feet which literally tore the big canine to shreds.

Another wolf sprang to the attack, snapping at the stallion's nimble heels. The stallion kicked savagely, catapulting the wolf thirty feet, and caving in the ribs. The big horse then jumped on the crippled wolf and battered him with the sharp front hoofs until he was dead.

The rest of the wolf pack retreated to a safe distance as the stallion faced them defiantly. The horse whistled angrily at the mares, ran at them with snapping teeth to give weight to his orders, and drove them after the main herd.

The wolf pack drew closer as the big stallion guarded the rear of the now running mares. A dozen young colts had been killed, and the ravenous wolves began to feed just as the last light faded from the dull sky.

Racky stirred and then stretched lazily. It was an ill wind that brought no benefits to someone, and Racky knew that the coyotes would be attracted to the kill out on the far-reaching plains.

Ricky retreated into the large hole, watching her mate. Racky was licking his hands, a sure sign that he was hungry. When enough time had elapsed for the prowling coyotes to be attracted to the slain animals, Racky chattered gently at Ricky and began to climb down.

It would be a good night for the hunting of mud turtles. The rains had roiled the deeper pools which abounded along the course of the brawling creek. But first there were quail eggs to start their evening meal, and the blue elderberries would furnish dessert.

Ricky was more emotional than her matter-of-fact spouse. The killing of the whistling swan had left an indelible impression on her feminine mind, and she shuddered as she remembered the slaying of the young horses. These things were more real to her than they were to Racky, who looked upon life as something to be retained by the practice of eternal vigilance.

Racky was alert as he crept through the undergrowth, with Ricky at his heels, in search of quail nests. He would leave the daydreaming to Ricky, and she seldom went hunting without him. He chattered softly when he found a nest with three eggs in it, and after taking one for himself he left the other two for Ricky.

It was now very dark in the underbrush, and Racky ambled along with his nose tilted to catch every vagrant scent. After robbing another nest, he led the way to the brawling creek where turtle eggs would be easier to find after the rain. The rains had also brought out a multitude of toads,[5] which hopped about licking up water beetles,[6] and stinkbugs.

5. *Bufo nestor* Camp
6. *Dytiscus marginicollis* Le Conte

Ricky came quickly to Racky when a long wavering cry shrilled eerily through the moist night air. He reassured her with a lick or two of his tongue as he recognized the cry of the cowardly coyote—as though he were trying to tell her that all the animals must have food to sustain life, even as they themselves were hunting. The eternal feminine, and the masterly male, living the simple elemental life of La Brea, not so long ago as measured by geologic time.

Forty thousand years is a mere pinpoint of time in the great scheme of things. Ricky, however, was living for the present, and the battles among the predators always frightened her. Racky was made of more sturdy stuff, and, like most males, he left the refinements to the more gentle sex. At the moment he was busy turning an unwary mud turtle on its back. He knew that when he had broken the shell and had extracted the toothsome meat, Ricky would wash her hands daintily and join in the feast.

10. The Miracle of Life

Nature was shifting her pawns about on the great chessboard of the universe. As the great glacial packs moved ever closer to the south, vast migrations of animals were traveling before that slow steady advance. The animals represented in this vast migration were legion.

Huge herds of horses and bison were drifting south, living on the country, and leaving their skeletal remains as mute evidence to be found thousands of years later. Giant sloths lumbered along, with their lesser relatives, the smaller ground sloths. Antelope and deer were abundant, as well as several species of bears.

Great condors and eagles filled the skies, many forms of falcons and hawks, with waterfowl too numerous for any accurate census. Yet each had its place in the scheme of things, and in that delicate balance which nature always maintains.

The great carnivorous predators were very numerous. The lionlike cats, saber-tooth cats, lynx, foxes, coyotes, wolves, and the bear families, of which the great short-faced bear was the largest and most powerful.

Plant life was profuse in the semi-arid regions of Southern California, and there was abundant graze for the ruminants and herbivores.

As the great migration moved south—and this required thousands of years—the physical aspects of many of the animals changed to meet the new conditions they encountered.

Down through the uncounted ages, little *Eohippus,* the dawn horse, had changed from a tiny four-toed creature, no larger than a small dog, to *Equus occidentalis,* the Western horse, with one toe on each foot, or the hoof as we know it today.

In all this vast progression of evolution and change, *Procyon lotor,* the raccoon, seems to have remained the same. Perhaps the raccoon was more adaptable to changing conditions, and, being omnivorous, his diet was of course varied.

Thus it is that down through all the many ages since antiquity, the sage of the ages has left a record for the students of nature to observe and report. The raccoon left his footprints in the sands of time, in the geological formations of the earth's strata, in dry caves, but never in the tar pits that were the last resting places of so many of his more powerful contemporaries.

Was this because of his inherent love of cleanliness, his superior intelligence, the well-developed sense of smell, or a combination of all three? Nature alone knows the answer; we can only conjecture.

The rainy season had passed, and the lush grass had grown profusely. Underground water sources had been replenished, and a foot or more of water covered the viscid asphalt of the tar traps, camouflaging the hidden death that lurked beneath.

Up on the higher ground, where Racky and Ricky were now thoroughly at home, the air was sweet and clean for the most part, because of the prevailing winds which blew from northwest to southeast.

Racky crouched in front of his home, enjoying the warmth of the late afternoon sun. Ricky was doing her house-cleaning, and of late she had been growing a bit petulant and cross. She no longer snuggled close to her spouse, with her head resting lovingly on his shoulder.

A small group of antelopes[1] were grazing out on the plain, not far from the stream of running water. Among the trees to the east a herd of deer[2] were feeding on the low foliage of the bushes. Racky watched with his head cocked to one side. He observed the antics of several small fawns, and the jealous guardianship of the nervous does. The antlered bucks stood guard against any surprise attack.

Racky yawned and stretched luxuriously. The long twilight was fading into darkness, and it was time for the night's hunting.

Racky cleared his throat and glanced inquiringly at Ricky. He jerked his head toward the opening, but Ricky shrugged and settled down in the far corner.

Racky stared for a moment and then ambled over to sniff inquiringly at his mate. Ricky snarled back her lips, growled low in her throat, and indicated that she would rather be alone, and would not accompany her spouse on his nocturnal search for food.

Racky reminded her of the new quail eggs in the thicket below, mentioned that the turtles were again laying eggs abundantly, and that he knew a fine place where crayfish could be had for the taking. To all of which Ricky only grunted and covered her face with her thick white-and-black tail. Like most males, Racky could take a hint. He knew when he wasn't wanted, but he wisely held his tongue. Ricky

1. *Breameryx minor* Taylor
2. *Odocoileus*

had been snapping at him for more than a week, and she was taking less exercise.

Pondering on the unpredictable ways of the opposite sex, Racky crept from his home and lowered his muscular body to the ground. A night out by himself would be good for him, and Ricky would appreciate him more after staying by herself for a while.

Racky grunted softly and crept into the thicket where the quails nested. He soon found a pair of eggs, ate them with gusto, and licked his hands. He decided to try out the new fishing grounds by himself.

After satisfying his thirst at the brawling creek, Racky went to a deep pool and hovered above a shelving rock. Then his right paw darted down and clutched a fat crayfish. He enjoyed several of the delicious crustaceans, and then ambled into a thicket where the blueberries grew in profusion. This would be his dessert, and the night was still young.

A twig crackled off to one side, and Racky went up a tree like a gray streak of dull light. Snapping teeth clicked just below Racky's heels as he crept to an overhanging branch and glared down at a hungry coyote. He snarled defiantly at the disappointed canine, and then he sobered. He had been worrying about Ricky and her neglect of him and had not kept his mind on taking care of himself.

The tree extended out over the brawling creek and after taunting the coyote for a while Racky crawled to the farther end and dropped lightly to the ground. He made his way leisurely to another tree, with the infuriated coyote yelping and leaping on the opposite bank.

A huge lean shadow leaped at the coyote and sent it howling away with a slash in the shoulder. Racky went up the big tree when he recognized a male dire wolf, which bayed at the higher branches for a time, then trotted away.

But Racky was not deceived. He kept to his perch and waited until the wolf tired of his deception. When at last the wolf disappeared in the direction of the tar traps, Racky crawled again across the creek on the overhanging branch and dropped to the ground.

He reveled for a time in his newly found freedom, and then he began to grow restless. Perhaps Ricky was over her pouting now, and then again, something might be trying to get into their home. At any rate, his hunger had been satisfied, and he would take a pair of fat mice home for Ricky.

Racky ambled along, every sense now fully alert. Like most males, he didn't like to carry packages, so he hunted in the thicket just below his home. He saw a pair of kangaroo mice before they saw him, caught one in each hand, and snuffed out their lives. Then he started for his tree. Perhaps Ricky would not be so cross when she saw the peace offering he was bringing. If there was anything Ricky liked better than a nice fat mouse, it was another helping of the same.

It lacked an hour until daybreak when Racky climbed the tree and paused at the entrance to his home. He cocked his head to one side to listen and smell, and then he stiffened.

A strange sound came from the deep hollow. Perhaps something had happened to Ricky, and he was sorry he had stayed so long. If anything had happened to Ricky, he would never forgive himself.

He leaned forward and sniffed a long time. He could detect no strange odor, but again he heard a whimpering sound. Snarling a challenge, Racky crept into the hole and chattered a question.

His answer came instantly in the form of an answering snarl. But it was the voice of his beloved, and Racky crept closer.

Ricky was crouching in the farthest corner, glaring at him with red luminous eyes. She snarled and spit angrily, and Racky stared at his mate with disbelief. Then he slowly offered a mouse, which was snatched from his hand ungraciously.

Racky reasoned that as long as Ricky was hungry there couldn't be much wrong, and he slowly offered the other mouse. This was also snatched from his grasp, and as he stared to ascertain the reason for Ricky's hostility, Racky suddenly stiffened.

Something was moving beside Ricky. Perhaps it was a snake which had crawled into their home, but he could not detect the odor of a reptile. Then he saw the movement again, and he leaned forward curiously.

Ricky snarled and snapped at him, and Racky drew back to avoid her sharp teeth. Then a great light dawned on him, and he began to chatter noisily.

The movements beside Ricky were several wriggling little mites of pink flesh. They were calling softly, and Racky's chest swelled with pride. He was a father, but why hadn't Ricky told him of the impending miracle? He shrugged with resignation, and he talked softly in his throat, telling Ricky that she was the best mother in the world and asking her what she would like to have to eat—telling her just to name it, and he would go right out and get it for her.

Ricky answered more gently and allowed her lord and master to inspect the four new babies. But she would not allow him to touch the youngsters, and after watching them squirm for a while Racky said he would go and get her some food.

The raccoon clambered down the tree rapidly, filled with a new sense of importance. There were four new mouths to feed in the high bungalow, and he was just the proud father who could provide for his family.

Again he caught a pair of mice, but when he returned to his home and tried to give one of the mice to the baby raccoons, Ricky snarled at him viciously. She snatched the mouse and devoured it hungrily, telling her spouse that she would feed the babies, and to get on with his hunting.

Racky looked hurt, but he went down the tree again. He returned with a half-grown squirrel and settled down to watch Ricky dress the morsel. Now the four babies were quiet, and Racky watched and wondered about the miracle of life.

He had seen death in its most violent forms and had learned how to avoid hidden dangers. Then he remembered the small fawns and the newly born colts. He also remembered that spring had come to La Brea, and with its coming had also brought a perpetuation of all the species of life.

As the first light of the approaching dawn showed against the eastern sky Racky crept deep into his home and sank to rest beside Ricky and his family. Ricky chattered gently and laid her head across his shoulders, telling him to be careful and not to crush the babies. That which he had once seen, Racky would always remember. Now he felt entirely contented. He was a family man, and this . . . was the miracle of . . . life.

11. The Greatest Tragedy

The sky above La Brea was gray, and the air seemed to be filled with fine particles of dust. The westerly winds brought the fine ash and dust particles from across the wide Pacific. Somewhere, perhaps many thousands of miles away, great volcanoes were erupting, and the trade winds were carrying the minute particles of volcanic ash across half the world.

More significant was the effect these clouds of dust were having on the atmosphere. So dense were the clouds in certain areas that the life-giving rays of the sun were shut off from the earth. Without this warmth the air masses became increasingly cold.

Huge bodies of water were turned into ice, which did not melt for thousands of years, and these great bodies of ice were moving slowly southward, but with irresistible force. This brought about the condition we know as the Ice Age, and caused the migrations of the animals. They moved south well in advance of the glacial packs, seeking a more temperate climate where food and forage could be found.

Many of the great animals fled before the icy blasts which brought death to all living creatures and destruction to the natural foods on which they all depended for subsistence. The great ice packs also preserved the remains of unfortunate animals which were trapped. Vegetation has been found in the stomachs of some of these prehistoric creatures; grasses and leaves which had been eaten perhaps forty thousand years ago.

As the glacial ice moved southward the migrations of the animals increased. Some wandered over into Asia, using a great land bridge which connected what is now eastern Siberia with the North American continent, at far away Alaska. Others of the same species continued south into our own western states. Many continued the pilgrimage across still another land bridge, the one that connects North and South America. The camels of Asia, the llamas of South America, offer striking proof of this migration. The skeletal remains of camels found in the tar pits of La Brea provide the connecting link and the indisputable proof of the relationship between the *Camelidae* of three continents.

The great lands to the north were masses of frozen ice in which all animal and plant life had been destroyed. But all of life was struggling for existence, and in this case was being expressed by the great migrations, of which the astute raccoons were a very small part.

Racky crouched in the front of his home in the late afternoon, studying the dust-laden air with puzzled eyes. Ricky was caring for her family in the rear of the tree home. The four cubs were now covered with a coarse brownish-gray pelage and were becoming increasingly active. At times Ricky was exceedingly irritable. They seemed to be always hungry, but Racky was a mighty hunter and a good provider.

Whenever Ricky left the tree for exercise or to do a bit of hunting on her own, Racky seized the occasion to teach the small fry some measure of discipline. He would cuff them smartly if they did not come away from the opening when he spoke sharply. If the cubs were crying when

Ricky returned from the hunt, Racky would quickly leave the old homestead and clamber down the tree trunk to escape from her maternal wrath.

Today Racky stared at the dust-laden sky, and shivered slightly against a chill wind which was blowing from the northwest. He sniffed inquiringly when a distant trumpeting came down the wind. He could detect a strong musky odor, a smell with which he was only vaguely familiar. It was similar to that of the mastodon which had been trapped in the lake of tar. The raccoon stared toward the north, and his eyes widened when a herd of strange creatures appeared against the distant horizon.

Racky called to Ricky and made room for his mate when she crowded close to see what had caused his agitation. Ricky gasped at the strange apparition, closed her eyes, and looked again. The strange creatures were still outlined against the sky, and now they loomed larger as they thundered toward the water they could scent in the pools.

The two raccoons crouched in the doorway of their home, watching the thundering advance, scarcely daring to breathe. Other animals were attracted by the bellowing stampede, but they moved quickly out of the way to avoid being trampled under those tremendous feet.

Racky stared and leaned forward a trifle. Ricky drew back as she watched, and then both remembered having seen the lumbering animals in the north, during their southward trek. These were the huge Emperor mammoths,[1] the largest creatures of the Pleistocene era. Some of them were more than thirteen feet high at the shoulders and weighed seven or eight tons. Heavy tusks protruded from the upper jaws, extending in front of the powerful trunks for a distance of eight feet in some of the older male elephants, or bulls. The tusks, curved

---

1. *Archidiskodon imperator* Leidy

to overlap each other in a circle, served as a battering ram with which they could push over a tree of considerable size. Their great pillarlike legs terminated in three huge horny toes, with a treading surface the size of a small tub.

It was small wonder that all the lesser creatures gave the right-of-way to the stampeding elephants which could crush even the great short-faced bear under those tremendous feet. Thick tough hides encased the huge bodies, gray in color, and as thick as heavy armor.

There were perhaps as many as forty pachyderms in the stampeding herd, and the ground trembled as they lumbered toward the pools at a surprising rate of speed for creatures of their great bulk. Several baby mammoths ran beside their mothers, and it was these which would attract the attention of the skulking carnivorous beasts.

Evidently the elephants had been long without water, and they were traveling with the wind, which was now blowing from north to south. This prevented them from catching the odors from the tar pits, which were now well covered with water from the recent heavy rains. The beasts thundered to the west of the grove of live oak trees in which the home of the raccoons was located, toward the pools which gleamed invitingly under the leaden sky. They left a trail of broken trees and trampled underbush in their wake, and the creatures of La Brea were following in that wide wake, paying little attention to one another.

This was something the like of which few of them had ever experienced. This great storehouse of living flesh would provide food for many a day, in quantities hitherto unheard of.

Huge tawny forms appeared in pairs as the lionlike cats took the lead in following the unsuspecting victims. Dozens of saber-tooth cats slunk along through the brush, their sharp tusks gleaming in the eerie light of the early dusk. Dire wolves bellied low to the ground, their heads held low and forward, and hundreds of coyotes were assembling from the nearby hills.

Racky watched from his lofty perch, and he saw the main body of the elephant herd splash into a large pond. Sheets of water were flung high by the tub-sized feet as the momentum of their rush carried the mammoths in the lead far out into the pool.

The spray died down, and now there came a bellowing chorus of terror as the elephants began to sink down into the treacherous tar of the deceptive pools. A score were mired in the large pond, and here and there in smaller pools Racky could see the thrashing trunks of other unfortunates.

In the pond one bull was trying to wade to the opposite bank. His long trunk was waving furiously, but now he was in the tar up to his belly. The circular tusks were black with the viscid tar, and he could find no footing for his lunging front feet.

A second bull bellowed with fright as he struggled to escape. He was directly behind the leader, and he rested his spread of tusks on the leader's rump. Using the leader for leverage, he raised up and freed his front feet momentarily from the sucking trap. The leader, meanwhile, was pushed down by the weight on his back and was trampled from sight. The second mammoth, however, was also sinking lower and lower. The front legs slipped from their precarious footing, and the doomed elephant sank into the hole he had enlarged.

Ricky had retreated to the back of the tree home, but Racky crouched tensely as he watched the greatest tragedy of La Brea. One female elephant had been unable to crowd into the pool, and only her front feet showed where she had taken a first step. She now retreated

with her baby at her side, staring at the sinking bodies of her less fortunate companions.

In other pools under the cypress trees Racky could see the death struggles of other pachyderms. He could also see the Teratorni stirring sluggishly, and the air above the pools of death was filled with winged scavengers. Through the dense underbrush and coarse grass all the predatory creatures were gathering in anticipation of the feast.

Racky shuddered and returned his attention to the female elephant and her calf. The mother mammoth had lowered her long trunk and had quenched her burning thirst. The baby mammoth was drinking slowly, its mother hovering over it protectingly.

A pair of lions skulked through the brush, keeping low to the ground. They were watching the baby elephant, whose skin would be less tough, and whose flesh would be more tender and succulent. Then the mother elephant sniffed the air and whirled to face the new danger.

12. Six-Ton Mother Love

The baby elephant continued to drink, sucking up water with its trunk, and then spraying the liquid into its capacious mouth. The female was urging the baby mammoth away from the pool, and slanting her body to offer protection from the crouching lions.

It was almost dark, and Racky climbed down his tree home and scuttled through the brush to find a better vantage place. Lions and wolves were already feeding at the smaller pools, and the raccoon stayed well back and climbed a tree from which he could see without being observed.

He saw a small tar trap where a single female elephant had mired down almost to her skull. A baby elephant had been slain near the margin of the treacherous trap, and evidently there had been a fight over the ownership of the kill. A saber-tooth cat had been destroyed, and two dire wolves were lying with their hindquarters in the tar.

It was not a pretty sight, and Racky shuddered as he watched the birds and beasts at their feasts. He crept out on a limb, high up in the cypress tree. From the south came an angry bellow.

The female elephant was standing guard over her baby, facing a pair of lions which crouched threateningly. The baby mammoth was terrified and sought protection under the belly of its mother.

With her hindquarters toward the pool to offer some protection, the elephant waved her trunk continuously. She trumpeted her anger and fear at the crouching lions, who in turn snarled savagely as they inched up ever closer.

The male lion suddenly left the underbrush and circled off to the left. The lioness moved up a bit, snarling at the bewildered elephant, who only turned her head to watch the stalking lion.

The entire area was alive with the sounds of life and death, of terror and hunger. Elephants were trumpeting with insane helplessness, while all the great predators were snarling and roaring with the desire to kill. Far back in the low hills and heavy brush the coyotes gave tongue in a shrill wavering chorus. A snapping to the right drew Racky's attention. He saw a pair of dire wolves standing on the half-submerged body of a great tusker. The elephant's head and front feet were deep in the slimy petroleum mire, but the hindquarters were on solid land.

The two wolves were attacking the hind legs, but the thick protecting hide of the mammoth defied their onslaughts. The male wolf slashed savagely at the back of the pachyderm, but his teeth slipped from the tough hide without making any impression.

Racky watched wonderingly. Here were tons and tons of meat, seemingly for the taking. Perhaps after the great vultures had worked on those tough hides for a day or so, aided by the desiccating effects of nature . . . ?

Once again Racky turned his head to watch the mother elephant protecting her baby. The male lion was off to one side, while the lioness tried to hold the elephant's attention by a simulated frontal attack. The lioness sprang at the baby elephant, stopped her leap, and drew back. The female elephant waved her trunk and trumpeted angrily. For a moment she was caught off guard.

The male lion leaped high into the air, and his hind legs struck lightly against the left side of the mammoth. Then he was up on her back, trying to dig in with his great claws. The mother elephant bellowed with terror and shook herself violently. The lion lost his balance and leaped as he was sliding from that tough sloping back.

The baby elephant trumpeted with terror and ran from under its living protection. Then the lioness sprang at the frightened baby, raking savagely with her razor-sharp claws.

The mother elephant reached down with her long flexible trunk, caught the lioness over the back and under the belly, and threw the snarling beast under her front feet. The mother elephant stomped twice with those huge pillarlike legs, unmindful of the tearing claws which ripped at the tough skin covering her pile-driving legs.

The baby elephant ran back to its mother, who took a step to the side. The lioness lay writhing in a death agony, with most of her bones broken. Now the female elephant faced the lion, waving her trunk, which was now lacerated and dripping with blood. She seemed unmindful of any pain to herself; her only concern was for the safety of her offspring.

The lion could now smell the blood of its mate and the muskier odor of the gore from the elephant's dripping trunk. His enraged roars brought other lions to investigate, and they slouched toward the belligerent female in a half-circle. Only her rear was protected by the oily pool, and some instinct warned her to make a stand where she was.

Racky watched, and at times he trembled, despite the safety of his high perch. The male lion was facing the big elephant, his canine teeth gleaming in his slavering jaws. The trampled lioness twitched and screamed just once more. By some sixth sense of the wild, the lion knew that his mate was dead. He threw back his head, roared thunderously, and charged the elephant, leaping straight at her twisting trunk.

Once again the baby elephant stepped out from beneath its mother's belly. The mammoth bellowed as the lion bit at her trunk, and caught it with his front paws while his hind feet came up to rip at it savagely.

The elephant reacted with explosive force as the ripping claws tore into her flesh. She swung her trunk down suddenly between her forelegs. One front foot stepped on the snarling lion and ripped him free of her bleeding trunk. The stunned lion tried to turn, but he was not quick enough.

The elephant moved her front feet back to throw the crippled lion toward her back legs, under her belly. Then the back feet moved up to kick the screaming cat against the front legs. With the lion caught between those four armored pillars, the elephant sank down and mashed the lion to death.

As the elephant lurched up to regain her feet, the lion pack sprang to the attack. She was literally covered with great cats as she pushed up to her feet, and her flexible trunk lashed out madly across her broad back. She seized one lion and hurled it to the ground with stunning force. Then she stepped on the creature as her trunk lashed around again to clear her back. Another lion was clinging to one of her legs, and she stepped on it with a quick backward move.

The mother elephant was now temporarily freed from her assailants, but the lion pack had gone insane with anger and injuries. A male

lion was on the baby's back, and the frightened baby mammoth bellowed with terror and ran under its bleeding mother. The lion was hanging on desperately, cuffing at the baby elephant's head and ears. The lion was brushed from the youngster's back as it ran under its mother, and a great tublike foot stepped on the lion's head.

Now the lion pack retreated, forming a circle around the embattled mammoths. The little elephant was moaning with pain, and the mother fondled it protectively with her bleeding trunk. Then she took her stand facing the snarling pack of lions, waving her long trunk from side to side and high over her towering head. On the ground around the battlefield four lions lay dead, smashed almost beyond recognition. These would furnish food for the scavengers.

Racky could hear the stirring of great wings in the trees closer to the pools. He could hear the yapping chorus of the coyotes in the near distance, raising high above the trumpetings from those entrapped mammoths which were still alive.

There were now other things to think about, and Racky climbed cautiously down from his high perch. The four cubs back in his own home had to be fed, and Ricky would be wondering about his absence.

The hungry raccoon satisfied his hunger at the berry patch near the brawling creek. He caught a crayfish and broke the soft shell. Racky returned to his home with a pair of fat mice for Ricky, climbed down again and found some quail eggs, and caught a young ground squirrel for the family.

The moon was high by the time Racky had satisfied the demands of his family. In spite of Ricky's demand that he stay home for the rest of the night, Racky growled something about quail eggs in the thicket below their home and climbed down the tree. Inwardly he was consumed with a great curiosity about the female mammoth and her baby. He cautiously retraced his steps to the vicinity of the tar traps, skirting around such places which offered no shelter.

Out on the great plains he could see a herd of bison grazing westward. He also saw several of the great mammoths which had evidently escaped the pools and had satisfied their thirst in the cool pure water of the creek. One great bull was plucking leaves from a bed of giant ferns, and the circular tusks gleamed white in the hazy moonlight. Occasionally the bull elephant would raise his trunk and trumpet loudly, evidently trying to call some of the lost females away from danger, for Racky heard an answering trumpet from the south.

He saw many skulking forms as he returned to the tar pits. The coyotes were drawing in closer, paying little attention to anything except the fresh meat they could smell at the death traps. One wandering coyote made a dash at Racky, who went up a tree, and snarled at the scavenger from the safety of a high perch. The coyote yipped a while and then joined his fellows, who were advancing stealthily toward the tar traps. After assuring himself that the way was clear, Racky climbed to the ground and continued his interrupted journey.

Keeping to the deeper shadows, he made his way to the tall tree and climbed aloft. He crept out on the long stout limb facing the tar pond.

The female elephant was still keeping her warlike vigil; the baby mammoth was lying on the trampled ground, under the belly of its mother. Most of the lion pack had fled from the scene of carnage, leaving their dead to the caretakers of nature.

Only three of the great cats remained to bait the mother elephant; these had probably lost their mates. They faced the pachyderm in silence, broken occasionally by a whining snarl as they stared at the trampled lions between the elephant and themselves.

Now the false dawn was threatening from the east, and one of the sentinel lions slunk away. A short time later another cat left the battleground, Racky still watched intently.

The baby mammoth stirred restlessly and lurched to its feet. The mother elephant bellowed and made a rush at the remaining lion. As the snarling beast retreated, the mother left the pond and began a slow and ponderous advance toward the north.

She raised her trunk and trumpeted inquiringly. Racky listened, and he heard an answering call. This he was sure came from the great bull elephant out on the plains.

With the baby close to her side, the mother elephant broke into a slow lumbering run. She kept to the wide avenue trampled down by the herd in its flight to water, and all the creatures of La Brea gave her the right-of-way. They had seen the devastation caused by those trampling feet.

Racky left the high tree and started for home. He arrived there just before the dawn, and he faced the coastal plains for a final look before retiring to sleep. Out against the distant skyline he could see the bull elephant with the huge spread of circular tusks. He could also make out the forms of several females, with their young under their front legs.

The raccoon turned his head slightly when a trumpeting call came from the southwest. Then he saw the female mammoth lumbering toward the creek, and the remnant of the herd. The baby was running at her side. As the tired elephants joined the herd, Racky yawned and crept to the back of the hollow in the high live oak tree. Mother love had triumphed again.

13. Thanksgiving Day at La Brea

The giver of light was shining brightly in the flawless sky. The air had cleared of the volcanic ash, allowing the warm sun to blanket the land once more with its life-giving rays.

A change had come over La Brea since the great tragedy of the mammoths. Two long days and nights had passed, and out in the smaller tar pits large islands had been formed by the partly submerged bodies of the imperial elephants.

Nature was working slowly to reduce the victims to their common elements; the vast skeletal remains would be preserved in the asphalt for posterity. The bones would be strangely intertwined with those of the predators which had sought to feed on them: lions and saber-tooth cats, dire wolves and coyotes, the great vultures and owls, and the lesser, gnawing rodents.

Man would come later—some thirty thousand years later. Meanwhile the great glaciers from the north would move steadily toward the south, and the migrations of the animals would continue before that inexorable advance.

Racky yawned and stretched his muscles as the warm sun sent an inquiring ray deep into his arboreal home. Ricky was talking possessively to the four mischievous cubs, telling them of the dangers of the great outside world. Racky listened indulgently, and then crept to the front door to have a look around.

A herd of horses was grazing out on the coastal plain toward the northwest. Beyond the horses was a larger herd of bison, their great humps silhouetted against the skyline. A pair of giant sloths were feeding in a copse of trees off to the east, and in a deep pool formed by the creek the remnant of the herd of mammoths were cavorting.

Racky watched the elephants with interest. The babies scampered ponderously, spraying water on one another. Two males stood guard, their tusks gleaming dully in the sunlight. The females were submerged in the cool water, recovering from the nerve-shattering experiences which had depleted their numbers with such devastating suddenness.

In a thicket of berries and shrubs Racky could see a small band of prong-horn antelope.[1] Waterfowl of various kinds were feeding in the small pools which were formed by the eddies of the creek, and high above, in the far ceiling of the turquoise sky, several Teratorni floated gracefully on motionless wings. Despite their great wingspread they now looked like tiny specks in the distance.

Racky knew that the great birds were watching the life, or the lack of it, at the tar traps. The Teratorni could glide on the air currents for as long as an hour without flapping a wing, and they possessed the keenest eyesight among the creatures which made up the Pleistocene assemblage.

Racky turned toward the south, and he studied the tar pits with

---

1. *Antilocapra americana* Ord

nose wrinkled to show his repugnance. Not that the odors bothered him as a usual thing, except when crosscurrents caused a shift in the wind. But the astute raccoon knew what would happen when time, and the elements, began their work of deterioration. Those mountains of flesh would rot and decay, and would finally return to nature in their component parts.

One of the raccoon cubs wobbled over to its father and tugged slyly at Racky's bushy tail. He moved it irritably, but the youngster was persistent. Racky reached around swiftly and cuffed the cub with his left hand, and Ricky upbraided her mate when the cub retreated with a whimper of injured feelings.

Racky stretched himself and paid no heed to the domestic yammer behind him. He was watching the thicket where the antelope were feeding. A number of large birds were feeding on the berries from the lower branches, and when he turned his head and sniffed the gentle breeze, Racky could hear a faint gobbling sound.

The birds strutted around the feeding grounds on long legs. They stood about two feet high, had fairly long necks, dull gray or bluish plumage, and were heavy breasted. These were the wild turkeys[2] of La Brea.

As Racky watched with renewed interest, a skulking gray form appeared at the far edge of the thicket. Racky recognized the gray fox, and leaned forward when the fox made a sudden leap and grabbed a turkey hen by one leg.

The startled turkeys half flew to the lower limbs of small trees as the captured hen squawked with terror. Her cries were soon ended when the fox dragged his victim into the brush and leaped on the hen to break her neck.

2. *Parapavo californicus* Miller

Racky nodded his head wisely. Here was a new source of meat-on-the-table for the taking, and he made a mental note to find out where the nests were located. There should be an abundance of large eggs. He called Ricky and indicated the new supply of food. Ricky licked her chops with anticipation, but Racky warned her that the other nocturnal animals would also be interested and that the utmost caution would have to be observed.

Ricky seemed duly impressed, and Racky swiveled his head around to study the thickets and coverts between his home and the tar traps. The ground seemed to be alive with the wild turkeys. Ricky pressed closer to see what had absorbed her mate.

It was the time of early twilight, and most of the La Brea inhabitants were astir. It was as though nature had issued an invitation to a sumptuous feast, and all who ran could read that unmistakable invitation. A saber-toothed cat seized a big gobbler and broke the neck with one swipe of a huge paw. A tawny lion pounced on a fat hen, and farther away, toward the north, even the cowardly coyotes were enjoying a feast of fresh meat.

A covey of turkeys broke from cover and crossed a clearing to get into the thicker underbrush. Instantly a pair of big hawks swooped down on the scuttling turkeys, struck viciously with their curved beaks, and came to earth to drag their victims into the brush.

Racky trembled with eagerness, but he restrained himself. He had marked the location of several bands of these ground birds, and when darkness enveloped the land he would know where to go for his supper. As though sensing his excitement, the cubs pushed forward and clamored to be fed.

Racky relaxed with a sigh of satisfaction. This task would keep Ricky occupied for a while, and after he had scouted the hunting grounds he would know if it were safe for Ricky to venture out on a hunt of her own.

The twilight faded and finally merged with the deep shades of night. Racky glanced over his shoulder. Ricky was curled up at the rear of their comfortable home. With a muttered grunt of farewell, Racky left the hole in the tree and clambered swiftly down the rough scaly bark.

He did not go to the thicket where the quail had their nests. He was after larger game this time, and he headed toward a thicket of berries not far from a bend in the brawling creek. Even in his haste to participate in the lavish feast provided by nature, the wise raccoon did not forget his native caution. He was well fleshed and in prime coat, and he had no intention of furnishing the meat course for some larger and more savage predator.

There was more to it than just catching a turkey. If he made his hunt close to the stream, he would not have to drag the bird any appreciable distance.

Racky reached the brawling creek and climbed a low cypress to reconnoiter. He waited on an overhanging branch, his sharp-pointed snout turned toward the berry thicket. With his ears tuned to catch every nocturnal sound, he crouched silently to watch and listen.

Racky stiffened slightly when he heard a faint gnawing sound. He remembered the kill of the gray fox, and he focused his narrow eyes on the spot where the fox had eaten its prey. Now he saw what had caused that gnawing sound; a pair of weasels[3] were feasting on the remains left by the fox.

Racky raised his head slightly and sniffed. A strong odor was

3. *Mustela frenata latirostra* Hall

becoming more pronounced, and that odor had the taint of very strong wild onions. A strange small animal with black-and-white stripes ambled boldly into the thicket, and Racky showed his displeasure when he recognized the striped skunk.[4]

Of all the animals of La Brea the skunk was the boldest. He did not yield the right-of-way for any of his more powerful contemporaries. When aroused to fright or anger, the skunk used a weapon more powerful than claw or fang. He could spray an obnoxious perfume for a distance of several feet, and the odor lingered for hours.

Racky watched the pair of weasels retreat hastily, leaving the half-eaten turkey for the skunk. Using every stealthy caution at his command, the raccoon lowered himself slowly to the ground, crept away from the thicket, and scurried to another thicket without arousing the militant skunk.

Now he crouched in a deep shadow and remained inactive for some minutes. He heard a stirring in the low branches of a scrub oak, and the restless cluck of a turkey hen. Still the alert raccoon made no move until he had placed his prey.

The hen was roosting just off the ground, on a limb not more than a foot high. Racky could see several other huddled shapes in a cypress tree, and now he had formed his plans. He bellied low on the ground to windward of the roosting turkey hen and began to inch his way forward. If he could stifle the hen's outcries, his chances of enjoying his feast would be greater. Little by little the raccoon moved forward until he was close to the scrub oak on which the sleeping hen roosted.

Racky kept his head low, and only his eyes turned upward to stare at the plump bird. He moved a trifle to the side, gathered his

4. *Mephitis mephitis* Mearns

powerful hind legs beneath his flanks, measured the distance carefully with the eyes of an expert.

The sleeping bird moved restlessly and slowly raised her head from a protecting wing. The raccoon made his leap, and his powerful right hand closed around the turkey's neck. The strong fingers gripped the windpipe to stop an outcry, and the raccoon jerked the hen to the ground and smothered the flapping wings with his body.

It was all over in less than a minute. The turkeys in the higher branches of the cypress tree did not leave their perches.

Racky backed away from the thicket, dragging the tender young hen toward the brawling creek. The turkey was soon reduced to a pile of feathers and glistening white meat. Racky disjointed a drumstick and washed it carefully in the clear water. He did not relax his vigilance while gorging himself to repletion.

Satisfied at last, he took the other drumstick for Ricky, knowing that she would probably make a hunt of her own while he acted as baby-sitter. Then he made his way through the thickets and across the rubble, always keeping to the shadows. He arrived home shortly after midnight. Ricky was waiting impatiently at the opening to their home, but she stopped long enough to take the turkey leg from his jaws. After sniffing it carefully to make sure that her spouse had washed the meat, Ricky took the edge from her appetite. Then she pushed past Racky and started on a hunt of her very own.

In any language, and in any land, plump turkey means the end of fasting, and the beginning of feasting. Thanksgiving Day had come to old La Brea.

14. The Land of Plenty

The warm days passed lazily in that fair land which was old Los Angeles long before the coming of man. There was food in abundance for all, and a corresponding decrease in personal battles between the savage predatory animals living at La Brea.

The lions and saber-tooth cats were sleek and well fed. The dire wolves and coyotes were no longer gaunt and ribby, and the vultures seldom left the vicinity of the pools. Even the bears had feasted sumptuously on the flesh of the huge mammoths and had grown fat and dull witted. Nature had supplied bountifully, and all the creatures of her creation had shared in that abundance.

The vultures had ripped the rotting hides from the great imperial elephants, and the bears had added the strength of their muscles and claws. Those mammoths which were not wholly in the tar traps were soon a mass of gleaming white bones. Some of the big elephants that had mired in the lesser traps were slashed and skinned by the Teratorni and by the three lesser species of vulturine birds. For a change of diet, the ground turkeys were comparatively easy to catch and provided meat for those carnivores which were not natural scavengers.

THE LAND OF PLENTY

There were also more sloths in the vicinity, although their natural habitat was more to the north and east in the desert regions, where yucca, Joshua trees, and other plants native to the extreme arid regions grew in abundance.

An occasional camel could be seen browsing among the trees near the brawling creek, and the remnant of the herd of mammoths had evidently decided to stop their southern migration for a needed rest.

Among the lesser animals life went on as usual. The rodents found not only food among the cavernous skeletons of the mammoths, but a refuge as well. The birds and insects shared in the gamy feast, and enjoyed at least a partial immunity because of the overabundant supply.

The horses and bison grazed peacefully on the great plains to the west, feeding on the bunch grass and natural browse. In the thickets the small antelopes enjoyed a temporary respite.

To this pastoral scene, something else had been added. The young of the various animals were frequently seen with their mothers, who guarded their offspring with a vicious jealousy.

Racky and Ricky had fed well the night before and had slept the entire day in their comfortable home high up in the old live oak tree. Racky was lying in the sun at the front of the roomy quarters, gazing lazily out over the peaceful land.

The cubs were now large enough to be troublesome. They wanted to get acquainted with the outside world, but Ricky was a wise mother and suggested patience. This advice was greeted with the usual resentment of the very young, and it was for this reason that either Ricky or her spouse usually blocked off the entrance.

Racky had become accustomed to the pestering of his brood, but he was quick with a correcting cuff when the tormenting became obnoxious. Now he stretched luxuriously, with that comforting feeling of well-being which comes to the healthy and well fed. With eyes half closed Racky contemplated life and found it good. There was still an abundance of quail in the thicket below his home. Crayfish could be had for the taking from under the flat rocks in the creek. Turtle eggs could be found if one searched diligently, and the stupid wild turkeys were very numerous.

Hackberries and the blue elderberries grew in profusion, and the young mice were now scampering in the underbrush. The rains had stopped, the sun was shining brightly, and there was an abundance of clear cool water from the creek and the many live springs.

Of course, life at La Brea was not all feast and pleasure. Eternal vigilance was still the price of surviving, but the raccoons were the wariest of all the La Brea assemblage. If he observed due caution and used the brains with which nature had provided him, a raccoon could expect to live to a ripe old age.

Racky raised his head when the wind shifted. His nose wrinkled inquiringly, and then he showed his distaste. The wind was blowing up from the tar traps and bringing with it an almost indescribable stench.

It had been a week since Racky had wandered down to the tar pools. Those islands in the pools were becoming less pronounced. The vultures had exposed the flesh of the mammoths mired in the asphalt, and time and the warm sun had aided materially in the deterioration.

Ricky coughed and came to the front of their home. Her nose wrinkled as the terrible odor assailed her delicate nostrils. Racky squirmed uneasily. Though they were far removed from the tar traps and Racky had wisely chosen a location off to the west, they both knew what was causing that terrible stench. The prevailing winds at their home were from west to east, but the west winds did not always blow.

This was one of those days when shifting crosscurrents had obeyed some obscure laws of nature. True to her sex, Ricky insisted that something should be done about it. Racky assured his spouse that the winds would change shortly, and a heated argument ensued. Ricky was all for packing up the children and heading for the seashore in the near distance, but, true to his sex, Racky did not relish a change from his accustomed habits.

It was less than ten miles to the ocean, but those ten miles would be fraught with danger. Food would not be so plentiful, and Racky argued that one had to take the bitter with the sweet. Ricky chattered and scolded and began to tidy up the cubs. Racky sulked at the mouth of the den, but now he wisely held his tongue. He was an old-timer at La Brea, knew all the choice hunting spots, and he liked the home in which he was living.

He glanced sullenly across the great coastal plains, and the ruff on his neck began to raise. He had noticed an absence of the lionlike cats around the tar traps, and then he suddenly remembered. The lions liked fresh meat when they could get it, and the decaying carcasses around the fleshpots of La Brea were repulsive to them.

Racky called Ricky and indicated with a thrust of his pointed ears. A pair of the tawny cats were stalking toward the feeding bison, sure evidence that the truce of abundance was ended.

The male lion was bellied low to the ground, watching a halfgrown bison calf. His mate waited in a covert of coarse bunch grass, with only the tip of her long tail moving.

Ricky shuddered involuntarily when the male cat tucked in his powerful flanks and leaped with devastating suddenness. The bison calf went down under the powerful bludgeoning of the lion's paw.

The big cat seized the kill and dragged it swiftly back into the high grass before the bison sentinel knew what had happened. Now the herd was on the move with rattling horns and clacking hocks, and the earth trembled under the stampeding of thudding hoofs.

Ricky watched the lioness disembowel the buffalo calf, and then both lions began to feed. Racky stared at the thundering herd, back to the feeding lions, and then he looked searchingly at Ricky. She trembled and crept back into her home. She cuffed an unruly cub, glared at the other three, and settled down in a compact ball, her ringed tail curled up over her eyes.

Racky stretched again and sniffed the air. The wind had changed again, from west to east, and the putrid odor was no longer noticeable. But Racky was not fooling himself. He knew the persistence of the opposite sex, and he also knew that with the days of warm sun the odor from the pools would increase in intensity. Perhaps a move in the near future was indicated, but he would delay that change as long as possible.

Not that he was afraid of Ricky, you understand. He was the boss in his home, and he had proved his dominance. Of course he had been helped by a change in the wind and the object lesson furnished by the hunting lions out on the plain. If he decided to move at all, it would be in the best interests of himself and his family. He'd wait and see, but in the meantime it would not hurt to look around and scout the territory to the west. It would be different if he himself decided that a change would be not only beneficial but desirable.

Ricky, curled up in the nest, slyly opened her eyes a trifle, her black-and-white ringed tail serving as a shield. She knew her lord and master.

She had planted a suggestion in his mind, and perhaps that seed would germinate and bear fruit. Meanwhile it would be best to maintain a discreet silence and let the lordly Racky believe that the thought of more pleasant quarters was entirely his own idea.

The sun sank to rest in the west, making a golden aureole out toward the blue Pacific. Then came the long twilight, and the ensuing period of dusk, when all of nature seemed to be in a state of temporary suspended animation. This was the hour of peace. The birds ceased their singing, and all the animals of La Brea rested. Even the west wind was still.

Ricky dozed peacefully while the shades of night shrouded the land. Racky stirred and then pushed to his feet. He left the nest without comment, climbed down the scaly bark, and stopped at the base of the live oak to look and listen.

He stirred restlessly when the wind shifted slightly and the hated odor of decomposed flesh again assailed his nostrils. He made a meal of quail eggs, gathered some hackberries, and ambled off in a northerly direction toward the brawling creek.

He had detected the fuzzy outlines of a stand of timber off to the west. It would be a long journey of reconnaissance, but the night was still young. Perhaps he would have a surprise for Ricky when he returned. He shuffled along, keeping to the cover of the bunch grass.

Once he was treed by a prowling coyote, and when the skulking scavenger had gone about more profitable hunting, Racky found himself in a tree not far from the great mammoths. The huge tuskers were standing guard over the remnant of the herd, their long circular tusks gleaming in the early moonlight.

Racky had never seen a creature so huge, and he crouched on a branch to make a close study. He identified the female which had fought so valiantly at the pond of tar. She was easily recognizable by the wounds on her trunk and front legs. The baby elephant, sleeping peacefully in a swale of lush grass, also bore the scars of battle.

Racky climbed down from his refuge and began his journey toward the west. It was nearing midnight when he reached the stand of trees. Here the air was clean and invigorating, and the trees were even larger than at La Brea.

15. Go West, Young Man!

Racky climbed a tall tree in the center of the woods which were west of the tar pits of old La Brea. He flattened out on a large branch to reconnoiter the surrounding territory from his aerial observation post. He tested the wind and sniffed with appreciation when no odoriferous taint marred its sweetness.

Thickets grew all about, and there was a small stream not more than a quarter of a mile to the north. From these outward signs the smart raccoon was sure of an abundant food supply. Crayfish and turtles in the stream, berries and quail in the thickets, and mice in the undergrowth.

Racky now began to study the trees, and his ears pricked forward as he saw one hoary monarch with a dark blotch, about twenty feet above the ground, on its main trunk. He quickly descended from his perch, made his way to the massive live oak, and climbed the scaly bark. After listening for some time at the large hole in the trunk, he made a careful investigation. The new apartment was even roomier than his old quarters, and after Ricky had done a bit of house-cleaning Racky was sure that she would approve of the new location.

Racky climbed to the higher branches in the great tree and found that he could see for miles in every direction. The air was sweet and clean and carried a salty tang from the ocean, which was not more than five miles to the west.

Eager to share his discovery with his mate, Racky climbed down the tree and began the cautious return trip to his old home. He did a bit of hunting to satisfy his hunger and to assure himself that the new location was even better than the old in the vital matter of an adequate food supply.

Racky thought of the distance he had traveled, and of the cubs which were not yet half-grown. The babies stayed with their mother for a year, during which time she taught them the habits of cleanliness, self-preservation, and the other numerous facts of life. The little fellows would have to make the journey in two stages, and Racky watched carefully for a tree which would provide a resting place approximately halfway between the old home and the new. He found an old tree near a clear sweet spring and then continued his homeward journey.

Ricky was waiting when Racky climbed the tree and crawled wearily into the nest. For a few moments she appeared indifferent, but Racky was not deceived. After eating the fat mice he had brought her, she seated herself close to the tired explorer and chattered suggestively.

Racky yawned and said he had been exploring the possibilities of new hunting ground. He added that now that the children were growing up, it might be wise to seek a more secluded neighborhood which was less fraught with danger. He alluded lightly in passing that the stench from the tar traps was not too pleasant, and Ricky nodded in perfect agreement.

With the ground work thus laid, Racky made his announcement. He told Ricky of the new roomy apartment in the old tree over in the west woods, reminded his spouse that the children would require two nights for the trip, and told her of the temporary sleeping quarters at the halfway location.

Ricky chattered with excited happiness, cuddled closer to the intrepid explorer, and assured him that they would be ready to start the next night. Racky swelled his chest with satisfaction, yawned luxuriously, and reminded Ricky that he had had a rather trying night. After which he curled his tail up over his muzzle and was soon sound asleep.

Ricky climbed down the tree and found a nest with three quail eggs. She made a hurried trip to a clear spring, drank deeply, gathered a few hackberries, and returned to her home.

The cubs were climbing over Racky when Ricky entered the tree home, and she cuffed them smartly and told them about the trip they were going to take. Racky slept through the domestic yammering, dreaming of the improvements he would make at the new home over in Westwood.

He awoke just as the sun was going down in the west, and he stretched and crawled to the entrance to enjoy the warmth. Ricky was close behind him, and the four cubs clamored for a chance to share in the family conclave. Ricky made room for the youngsters, and Racky cleared his throat, paused for a moment, and regarded his offspring sternly.

He told them of the new home, and of the dangers they might encounter en route. Then he called attention to the various animals out on the coastal plain.

The young raccoons were familiar with the horses and bison, the camels and the elephants. They had also seen the giant ground sloths and the lesser sloths. They knew the big dire wolves and the cowardly coyotes, and had seen the great vultures many times.

Racky turned to the south and studied the distant tar traps. A pair of lionlike cats were prowling in the aisle made by the elephants, and the youngsters shivered. Racky whispered and called attention to a pair of saber-tooth cats, and he ended his lecture of visual education with a stern warning to the cubs to stay close to their mother during the entire journey.

The two female cubs nodded solemnly, and Racky stared at the two boys. They were slightly larger than their sisters, and also slightly more adventurous. Racky warned them of what would happen if they attempted any side excursions on their own, and one of the boys laughed slyly behind his hand.

Ricky reminded her spouse that she had taken the youngsters on several short hunting trips, and added that all of them could climb a tree almost as fast as she could. The four cubs watched their father closely, and Racky smiled and said they'd do to take along.

The darkness of the night had closed in during the family discussion. Racky stretched to his feet and climbed down from the tree. He was followed by Ricky. And then the four youngsters made it a race for the ground.

Racky led his family to a clear spring and watched while the youngsters quenched their thirst. The oldest of the boys sprang on a young mouse, ripped the hide loose, and was getting ready to eat. He stopped when Ricky growled an admonition. The young raccoon obediently washed the morsel of food in the clear water. Racky caught a mouse for each of the girls.

The next stop was in a hackberry thicket, and Ricky warned the youngsters that this was no picnic, and not to make too much noise.

Racky chattered sternly and raced for a tall tree. The youngsters followed, and after they and Ricky had climbed aloft, Racky leaped high and began to climb just as a prowling coyote quartered close by.

When the scavenger had gone Racky was the first to descend, and he led the way through the thick undergrowth.

They reached the halfway tree shortly after midnight, and the tired youngsters lost no time in going to sleep. Ricky posted herself at the front of the deep hole in the tree, and Racky climbed down to do some more hunting.

He was attracted to a large thicket where the blue elderberries grew in profusion. He climbed a tree when he detected a familiar odor, and then he heard a loud grunting. A pair of huge grizzly bears were feeding on the luscious berries, and the big male grizzly growled a warning to his mate.

Racky watched as the two bears left the thicket, and then he saw the reason for their hasty departure. A great shaggy form appeared in a clearing, followed by another only slightly smaller. The short-faced bears sniffed at the spot so lately vacated by the grizzlies. Then they sat on their haunches and began to feed on the berries from the lower limbs. The male was almost ten feet tall when he reared up to reach a higher limb.

Racky watched the great bears feeding, and in a way he was glad. With the bears in the vicinity there would be less danger from the predatory cats, and the wolves and coyotes would also be inclined to seek other hunting grounds.

Racky descended quietly to the ground and returned to his family. He sought slumber just before sunrise, and it was late afternoon before the excited cubs aroused him from his sleep. The two boys complained of hunger, but Ricky cuffed them and told them to wait until their father said that it was safe for them to continue the journey to their new home.

The air was sweet and clean as the raccoon family watched the twilight shadows from their lofty perch. Racky chattered softly to call attention to a pair of short-faced bears in a nearby thicket. Ricky leaned forward with interest when two small bear cubs followed their mother, and Racky breathed a sigh of content.

He told Ricky and the youngsters that the bears would provide insurance of sorts from the wolves and cats, warning the two boys not to try to strike up a friendship with their very distant relatives, the short-faced bear cubs.

Night crept in swiftly, shrouding the land with its curtain of darkness, and the raccoon family began the second half of their journey. They skirted the berry patch, drank deeply at a small stream, and Racky showed the youngsters how to catch crayfish.

Ricky hovered over her brood, watching them catch mice, and she was lavish in her praise when the young raccoons washed their food before eating it. They traveled leisurely, reaching the woods where the new home was situated an hour before midnight.

Ricky chirped sharply when she missed one of the boys. Racky raised his head and counted noses. Then he began to move toward a thicket from which a low growling could be heard. He hesitated, then ran quickly to a thick oak tree, indicating to Ricky that she climb up with the other three children. Racky then ran to the thicket and climbed a small tree.

His heart almost stopped beating when he saw a pair of enormous grizzlies feeding on hackberries. Over in a small clearing a pair of grizzly cubs were cuffing at each other. Racky now saw his missing son: the eager youngster was watching the playful bear cubs and calling in his own tongue.

Racky was about to call to his son when he saw a movement in the brush behind the bear cubs. A tawny lion was watching the playing cubs and getting ready for a leap. Racky's blood turned cold, but he acted swiftly. He snarled loud and savagely, with all the strength of his lungs.

The startled cat hesitated, and then the brush was trampled as the mother grizzly crashed to the rescue of her young. She caught the lion with a swipe of one huge paw just as the cat started his delayed leap. The blow sent the cat sprawling, and he roared with pain and beat a hasty retreat. The mother bear ran to her cubs and cuffed them soundly.

Racky dropped to the ground and went to meet his wayward son, who was whimpering with fright. Racky snarled and slapped the youngster smartly. Then he led the way to the great oak tree and told the terrified youngster to start climbing.

Ricky was waiting in the new home, and she greeted the prodigal with another sound cuff. The opening was darkened as Racky crept into the roomy hole, and he watched for a moment as Ricky licked the frightened youngster with her long red tongue and gathered him to her with maternal love.

Racky turned and crouched in the opening, to look down at the ground. The pair of grizzlies were looking up and growling savagely. Racky made no answer as he wondered whether they were welcoming him and his family to Westwood or blaming his son for getting their children in trouble.

After a time he found his voice and thanked the mother grizzly in his own way, telling her that perhaps someday he would do as much for her cubs and assuring her mate that his children would cause them no more trouble.

The male grizzly growled in his throat and rubbed a huge shoulder against the thick tree. Racky could feel a tremor run through the trunk, and he sighed with relief when the grizzlies called to their two cubs and ambled off in search of more food.

The night was still now except for the hum of insects and the occasional call of a hunting owl. It had been a long and dangerous trip, and Racky was glad that the journey was over. He hoped that Ricky would like their new home and that they could settle down and raise their family without any more house-hunting.

Ricky joined him in the doorway, and they watched the sun come up in the east to announce the birth of a new day. The children were sound asleep in the rear of the roomy apartment, and Ricky cuddled close to her spouse and laid her head across his broad shoulders.

Perhaps they talked in whispers of an education for their youngsters; Ricky would see to that. Thousands of years later, when men would come to California, they would find a record of Pleistocene life in the tar pits of La Brea. The world would know about the great migrations that linked the Ice Age with recent times.

Racky settled down and purred with contentment. He had no way of knowing that a great university would one day be built on the very spot where he and Ricky had located their new home. He did know that the air was sweet and clean and that life was good.

In that dim future, man would find the tar pits of La Brea. With all the skill and knowledge known to science, the indelible records would be taken from the pits where they had been preserved down through the ages.

Addenda: The La Brea Excavations

In 1875, on the ranch of the late Major Henry Hancock, the bones of extinct animals were first discovered. They were in the tar pits, from which asphalt was being taken for commercial purposes. These skeletal remains were first described by William Denton in 1905, and the importance of the tar pits to science was first recognized by W. W. Orcutt and Frank M. Anderson, who recovered some of the fossilized bones. Dr. John C. Merriam of the University of California directed the first excavations in 1906.

The ground surrounding the pits was solidified. Boxes and boards were placed on the asphalt in the pits, covered with layers of burlap on which the scientists found a footing, and added to as the first layers sank beneath the asphalt.

The average depth of the productive pits was twenty-five feet below the surface of the ground. Some of the pits or pools were formed by "fills" as the overflow escaped to natural pockets or depressions.

It was necessarily a messy business. The bones were all mixed together, and widely separated owing to the movement of the oil beneath the asphalt, volcanic disturbances, and earth tremors. The underlying stratas were of blue and brown clay, sand, and solidified asphalt. The bones were removed and taken to the Los Angeles County Museum, where they were later cleaned with detergent chemicals, studied and identified, and later assembled to provide the exhibits you see today in the Hancock Room.

This work was later directed by Dr. Chester Stock, now Senior Curator of Science at the Museum. In one pit, a mass comprising less than four cubic yards that was recovered by Dr. Merriam contained fifty heads of dire wolves, thirty skulls of saber-toothed cats, and numerous heads of bison, horses, sloths, coyotes, and birds. Remains of the predatory animals were preponderant.

As the scientists toiled in the pits, carefully digging out the skeletal remains, the pattern of the survival of the fittest became apparent. If a horse was trapped, the cats and wolves gathered to feast, to fight, and to devour one another. The victims, the victors, and the losers were all entombed and preserved together. Their bones were deposited on top of each other.

As the scientists, working on their makeshift platforms of boards and burlap, disinterred the skeletal remains, other men of science were cleaning the bones of the smelly asphalt. These bones were later identified and assembled, a labor of years. Many more extinct animals remain in the pits as a proof of the cycle of birth and death which covered many centuries.

In 1915 Mr. G. Allan Hancock gave to the County of Los Angeles the tract of twenty-three acres which now comprises Hancock Park. The pits have been surrounded with stone walls, and the exudation of oil and asphalt still continues and can be observed by the public. Lesser tragedies still occur, when squirrels and small birds become entrapped, as a grim reminder of what happened there, thousands of years before the coming of man to Southern California. Statuary groups have been erected near the pits in Hancock Park, giving mute but unmistakable proof that back in the Pleistocene era forty thousand years ago . . . "Animals were GIANTS in those days!"

CHARLES M. MARTIN